SHACKLETON
A LIFE IN POETRY

SHACKLETON
A LIFE IN POETRY

To Carol
with best wishes

JIM MAYER

Jim Mayer

Signal

Signal Books
Oxford

MV ORTELIUS ANTARCTICA 2015

First published in 2014 by
Signal Books Limited
36 Minster Road
Oxford OX4 1LY
www.signalbooks.co.uk

A catalogue record for this book is available from the British Library

ISBN 978-1-909930-10-0 Paper

Cover Design: Tora Kelly
Typesetting: Tora Kelly
Cover Images: Alex Gunn/State Library of Victoria/Wikimedia Commons; US Navy Military Sealift Command
Half-title image: Vincent van Zeijst/Wikimedia Commons

Printed and bound in Great Britain by TJ International Ltd, Cornwall

"When combined with great physical strength, and with powers of leadership, a poetic nature such as Shackleton's is the very stuff from which the greatest explorers are made."
James Mann Wordie, *Geographical Journal*, 1922

"Browning will never fail him,"
The Times, 17 September 1921

Of Browning's poem "Prospice":

"For many years we used it in telegrams as a code to breathe courage when parted in the hope of reunion. The last two lines gave me hope in the darkest days of loneliness and are still to me like a beckoning hand."
Emily Shackleton, December 1922

CONTENTS

INTRODUCTION:
POETRY IN ACTIVE LIFE

1911

Members of the Poetry Society gathering in central London for their October meeting eagerly anticipated that evening's charismatic speaker, the dashing explorer Sir Ernest Shackleton.

Just three years previously, he had turned his back on the South Pole, only 97 miles short of his goal. He later told journalists that "Death lay ahead and food behind, so I had to return."[1] Since then he had been lecturing on both sides of the Atlantic and in Europe, but speaking to an audience of poetry lovers might have seemed an unusual engagement for the 37-year-old, steely-eyed explorer. He modestly told the audience that "his only claim to talk on the subject was his appreciation of poetry and its teaching."[2]

In fact, Shackleton had a life-long affinity with verse. He often quoted poetry on his expeditions, to bolster, inspire and consol, both himself and his team. He was known to have crafted his own poems too. Thus, as an Antarctic celebrity and poetry aficionado, he was an ideal speaker for the Society.

Shackleton took to the platform to give his lecture entitled "Poetry in Active Life" and joked with his audience that they were the second smallest group he had ever spoken to. *The Times* of 28 October suggests that he got away with it, "putting his small audience in good humour" before explaining how sailors and explorers were "trained by their everyday life to feel what only poets can say".

*

There were many sides to Ernest Shackleton. Primarily a sailor and an explorer, he was also a failed parliamentary candidate, occasional journalist and one time City man. He was married with children but is known to have had extra-marital affairs. Shackleton's life was spent flitting, moth-like, between bright lights but his goal was constant: fame, and with it a steady income. He was prepared to try almost anything but exploring was the only occupation he felt he was good at. He ventured to Antarctica four times before his death aged just forty-seven.

Poetry was a constant thread running throughout this life of change and challenge from his cradle to the stone above his grave. As a boy, while truanting with his older friends from school in London, Shackleton inspired them with quotations from poems he had learnt around the family dining table of his childhood home. The day before his death he quoted Robert Browning in his diary:

Thankful that I can
Be crossed and thwarted as a man[3]

For Shackleton, to be challenged was to be alive. Each hurdle faced was another step on the way to making a name for himself. He used poetry for support, like a buttress as he clung to life and continued to command during difficult times in the Antarctic and harder times at home. Reading and writing poetry was vital mental maintenance.

As an incisive leader, he also realized that the wide horizons his sailors and explorers experienced would make them receptive to the poets' rhetoric and imagery. He used poetry as a tool, to encourage, control and motivate men who were frequently operating close to their physical and psychological limits.

Back at home, the books and lectures which funded his expeditions were perfect outlets for Shackleton's personal library of poetic quotations as he sought to conjure up the atmosphere, perils and emotions of his exploits 8,000 miles away in Antarctica to an audience in a fashionable, warm London hotel.

2011

The screen behind me swings so wildly that I'm not sure how my audience can continue to look at it. Our ship is ten times the weight of Shackleton's *Endurance* and yet the Southern Ocean treats us like a cork. One of the things I love most about my work is finding new ways to bring the heroic age of exploration to life for our passengers, and on this occasion as we lurch southwards I am giving a lecture entitled "Poetry at the Poles".

This book has grown from my research for that lecture. Almost every heroic explorer seems to have quoted poetry from time to time but the more I dug into Ernest Shackleton's papers and life, the more examples I found. It seemed that for Shackleton, poetry was not just for show, but was at the very core of who he was.

It has been an exciting journey through archives, biographies and correspondence, some unpublished until now. This literary treasure-hunt has run alongside my own professional voyages to South Georgia, Elephant Island and into the Weddell Sea. These contrasting journeys—one dry and dusty, the other cold and wet—have existed in symbiosis over the last two years, each contributing to the other and enriching my own appreciation of both poetry and Antarctic exploration.

Shackleton: A Life in Poetry is the result. It is a biography telling Shackleton's story through the verses he loved, his own compositions and the poems that his adventures inspired.

AUTHOR'S NOTE

Many of the lines of poetry discussed in this book are found among the handwritten letters and diaries of Ernest and Emily Shackleton. Ernest deployed punctuation only sparingly and

Emily's handwriting is awful. On occasions I have added words or marks for the sake of clarity and these appear in [parenthesis]. I have been sparing with the use of added marks or notes of [sic] in order that the verses do not become cluttered and remain readable. Lovers of the apostrophe you have been warned! I owe a debt of thanks to Regina W. Daly (*The Shackleton Letters*) and Michael H. Rosove (*Rejoice my Heart*) for carefully transcribing and publishing some of these letters, a task which greatly helps all Shackleton scholars.

All quotations used are referenced using a superscript number. The sources are listed by chapter at the end of the book. Quotations reproduced are faithful to the sources, which result in some idiosyncrasies of spelling and punctuation.

Throughout this book I refer to Shackleton's expeditions by the names of the ships they sailed in, rather than by their much longer expedition titles or dates. For clarity, here is a summary of the expeditions' formal titles, ships, leaders and dates.

DATES		SHIP	EXPEDITION TITLE	LEADERS
1901-1903	6 August to 28 February	*Discovery*	British National Antarctic Expedition	Capt. Robert Falcon Scott RN
1907-1909	7 August to 25 March	*Nimrod*	British Antarctic Expedition	Ernest Shackleton
1914-1916	8 August to 3 September	*Endurance*	Imperial Trans-Antarctic Expedition	Sir Ernest Shackleton
1921-1922	21 September to 16 September	*Quest*	British Oceanographic and Sub-Antarctic Expedition (also better known as the Shackleton-Rowett Expedition)	Sir Ernest Shackleton, until 5 January 1922. Thereafter, Frank Wild

1 THE JOURNEY OF ERNEST SHACKLETON

Before embarking on a journey through the life of Ernest Shackleton, navigating by the poems and poets which were central to that life, the next few pages present an overview of the complete voyage.

Ernest Henry Shackleton came of age on a square rigger rounding Cape Horn. Born on 15 February 1874 in Ireland, Shackleton attended school in south London, which diluted his Irish accent but did nothing to diminish his Celtic spirit. He was keen to go to sea, signing on to the *Hoghton Tower* in 1890, aged sixteen.

For the next eleven years Shackleton worked his way around the world on a variety of merchant ships, always accompanied by books of poetry, and progressing through the officer ranks. By the age of 26 he realized that attaining the rank of captain would not satisfy his ambition and, casting about for a new challenge, he applied to join Captain Scott's first expedition to the Antarctic on board *Discovery*, in 1901. This opportunity arose at just the right point in Shackleton's career, but not at such an ideal juncture in his personal life.

Emily Dorman shared Shackleton's love for poetry and had been the object of his affection since they were introduced to each other by his sisters in 1897. Emily in turn introduced Shackleton to the works of Robert Browning. Slightly older than Shackleton and intellectually his superior, Emily was a challenging prospect. As *Discovery* sailed, Shackleton received permission from her father for their marriage. This union would have to wait for his return, 24 months later, but it served to cushion Shackleton from a great disappointment.

Captain Scott sent Shackleton home early from the *Discovery* expedition. Shackleton had distinguished himself during the long polar winter, and was consequently picked by Scott as one of the three-man team to reach the furthest south, an ardous expedition which had a detrimental effect on the wellbeing of all three. On the advice of the two expedition doctors, Scott concluded that Shackleton's health was not up to remaining in the Antarctic for a second winter. A clash of characters had also developed between the two men whilst on the march. Although their return to the comfort of *Discovery* healed much of this division, reverberations of disagreement still echoed around McMurdo Sound when Shackleton returned in 1908.

Shackleton married Emily Dorman and they made the first of their many homes in Scotland. Their son Raymond was born soon thereafter. Between 1903 and 1907 Shackleton's restlessness led to a new job or project each year: secretary of the Royal Scottish Geographical Society, a prospective Member of Parliament, industrialist and entrepreneur. His excess of energy created difficulties at home and he embarked on a number of affairs of the heart.

Soon after the birth of their daughter Cecily in December 1906, Shackleton announced his intention to return to the Antarctic. Sailing on *Nimrod*, this time *he* would be in charge, right from the inception of the expedition. This major private expedition was to be mounted to the Polar Regions without the support of the scientific or naval establishment. Doing things "his way" brought Shackleton very close to success but not without raising some hackles along the way.

This was the first expedition to publicly state that the attainment of the South Pole was the primary object, and through sheer force of will Shackleton came tantalizingly close. He turned back just 97 miles from the pole. Perhaps just a few more days of struggle would have seen him at his goal, but for Shackleton there was nothing to be gained by dying while achieving the published aim. His contemporary Roald Amundsen rated this expedition as the single most important venture to Antarctica thus far.

Amundsen was not alone in his admiration; Shackleton received a hero's welcome on returning home in June 1909. He was awarded a knighthood by King Edward VII and embarked on a successful lecture tour.

As brightly as a star burns, so eventually will it fade and despite the birth of their third child Edward in July 1911, Emily described 1912 as the least happy of times. Shackleton's response to these emotional doldrums was to propose another project even more daring and spectacular than the last.

More than 5,000 men (and three Girl Guides) applied to join the Imperial Trans-Antarctic Expedition when it was first announced in December 1913. By that time, both of the poles had been conquered, but no-one had yet made a complete traverse of the Antarctic continent as Shackleton now proposed. Two ships sailed south in late 1914. *Aurora* laid depots from the known side of the Antarctic continent following the route towards the Pole that Shackleton had used before. Meanwhile Shackleton sailed in *Endurance* to the relatively unknown Weddell Sea side of Antarctica. It was a continent on which, as it turned out, he would never set foot again.

Pinched in sea-ice conditions described by the whalers as the worst they had seen for years, *Endurance* was carried further and further from land before being crushed and eventually sinking in November 1915. For almost six months, Shackleton kept up the spirits of his men as they camped on floating ice floes and drifted at the whims of the currents. He learnt that, as Napoleon put it, "a leader is a dealer in hope". Eventually they were able to launch their lifeboats as the ice broke up beneath their camp. Six days later, the cold, salt-stained party stepped onto land that was solid but far from dry, for the first time in 494 days. They had landed on the uninhabited Elephant Island. At this point, Shackleton left his men in the care of Frank Wild while he set about securing their salvation.

With five others, he sailed on an audacious 800-mile journey across the infamously stormy Southern Ocean in a small wooden

Endurance beset by the ice of the Weddell Sea
(Library of Congress, Washington DC)

lifeboat with the hope of seeking rescue for his marooned party. Sixteen days later, having had next to no sleep, Shackleton and the crew of the *James Caird* miraculously landed on the south side of the lonely island of South Georgia. The day was 10 May 1916, the start of the Antarctic winter. There was still one more uncharted obstacle between Shackleton and salvation; it was a challenge that no one had completed before.

The whaling station of Stromness on the north side of South Georgia was stocked with ships and men with which to mount a rescue. "The Boss" led his companions on the first ever crossing of the mountainous and glaciated interior, which he described as "a wracking march of 36 hours". Once at Stromness, it took Shackleton four attempts from three different countries over a period of three months to rescue his men from Elephant Island (all of whom survived). He had become a different man by the end of this expedition, and in May 1917 it was to a very different world that he returned.

The Great War was in full swing and Shackleton was anxious to have his part of the action. He undertook a variety of unsatisfying roles and never fired a shot in anger, returning to

Britain in July 1919 not knowing what to do with himself. He fell back into lecturing by default but was soon making further plans.

Shackleton's initial idea to venture to the Arctic and discover new lands in northern Canada came to nothing when the support promised by the government there did not materialize. He once again turned his sights southward and sailed in September 1921 on the ill-suited *Quest*, for lands that were already well charted. It was a sad reunion of old shipmates, rallying around their beloved leader and, for want of anything else to do, heading back to South Georgia. Shackleton's health had been fickle throughout his life, and now it finally failed him. He died on 5 January 1922 shortly after his arrival at South Georgia. He is buried on the hillside close to the former whaling station of Grytviken, with his head pointing to the south.

2 EARLY YEARS

When, in 1910, an interviewer "thinking that men of action were not always men of books", asked Shackleton if he read, his answer was blunt: "Always."[4] His mother claimed that this interest in books, and particularly poetry, was a result of her Irish heritage but she should not be allowed to take all the credit; for a particular family treasure was a poem handed down from the paternal side of the family:

> Dublin: The 10th of the 5th mo., 1734.
> Honoured Father,
>
> Since my last I've seen the Fair
> And many Tents and Drunkards there.
> Six foreign Beasts I went to see
> And Birds of which one frightened me.
> I've seen at last the mighty Sea
> And many ships near to the Quay.
>
> I've seen the College and the Castle
> And many boys that love to wrestle.
> With dearest love I now conclude
> And always hope I may be good.

Richard Shackleton, Ernest's great-great-grandfather, apparently wrote this verse when eight years old. Ernest's father Henry kept up the poetic tradition at home, with poetry recognition competitions around the dining room table.[5] Henry was a rather eccentric farmer and horticulturist turned homeopathic doctor, with a Quaker background and a passion for poetry. He encouraged all of his children to read, particularly the Bible and the works of poets far greater than Richard Shackleton, including

Tennyson, Macaulay and Longfellow. "Casabianca" (1826) by Felicia Dorothea Hemans was a favourite. It is easy to recite, and the sentiments of duty and obedience would have rung true in a Victorian upbringing. The familiar opening lines run:

> The boy stood on the burning deck
> Whence all but he had fled;
> The flame that lit the battle's wreck
> Shone round him o'er the dead.

Brought up initially in the country in County Kildare, Shackleton was educated at home with his brother and eight sisters by a governess, until they moved to England when Ernest was ten. His early prose reading often took the form of short stories in magazines such as *The Boy's Own Paper*. He was particularly drawn to tales of travel and adventure; Jules Verne was an early influence and he enjoyed *Twenty Thousand Leagues under the Sea*. He identified so strongly with the character of Captain Nemo that he later adopted Nemo as his own *nom de plume*.

Although a voracious reader, Shackleton was not a bookish boy, he also enjoyed the outdoor life. When the family moved to London in December 1884, he was sent to the Fir Lodge Preparatory School in Sydenham where his Irish accent earned him the nickname "Micky" (there was already a boy called Paddy). From there he went to Dulwich College as a day boy for two years. He was never a star pupil. Frequently involved in fights, he did not excel at sports, nor were his academic successes to be celebrated. Reflecting on his schooling he said, "teachers should be very careful not to spoil their [pupils'] taste for poetry for all time by making it a task and an imposition."[6]

Avid reading of adventure stories full of the Victorian spirit of Empire had a much greater effect on the ambitions of the young Shackleton than school. He remained a fan of Jules Verne and of books of his such as *The English at the North Pole* (1864) which trumpeted phrases such as "I will not allow, we will not allow, other people to have the glory of pushing further

Shackleton attended Dulwich College, London
(private collection)

north than ourselves..." and "...here is our country's flag, I am determined that these colours shall float upon the North Pole."

The influence on Shackleton is obvious, and he claimed that he was drawn at first not to Antarctica but to the north Polar Regions, gobbling up every book on the subject. This diet of expedition literature and his discomfiture at school fuelled an urge to get away to sea. He played truant with his friends to the bustling London docks but they failed to persuade any of the ships' crews to take them on as cabin boys.

Eventually, Ernest struck a deal with his father that, if he finished school, he would be allowed to go to sea. Immediately Ernest's school reports improved as he recognized the importance of mathematics to navigation. Aged sixteen, he set sail as a apprentice on a tramp ship of the North-Western Shipping Company. Tramp ships have no fixed itinerary and sail the world seeking and carrying cargoes, never knowing where they might be called on to go next.

*

Shackleton asserted in a magazine interview that going to sea marked the point that his education really started: "my first voyage taught me more geography than I should have learned had I remained at school to the age of eighty". He also bemoaned the forensic teaching of literature at school, claiming again to have learnt more at sea where "I seemed to get at the heart of it then, to see its meaning, to understand its message and in some degree to catch its spirit." Shackleton came of age as a reader too during these first hard years at sea. A. B. Cooper, the author of the magazine article, reckoned that "the elemental forces of school life are a great... training for a boy."[7] Shackleton stated that the wider, wilder elemental forces of the world experienced from the deck of a globetrotting ship were required for *his* education.

Commercial sailing was a school of hard knocks. Despite his father having secured his position through personal contacts, there were no special favours for the young Ernest. He would have been called upon at any time of the day or night and in all weathers to go aloft and change sail. This was work for, and amidst, the toughest of men.

After his death, a school friend from Dulwich College, Nicetas Petrides, wrote to the *Daily Telegraph* of these early years. Among stories of Shackleton falling overboard in some Asiatic port, not being able to swim and being rescued, Petrides remarked that it was unsurprising that there was a dearth of information and letters from Shackleton's early years at sea. This period was to be his "university", a key period in the formation of the man. Few undergraduates write home to reveal their experiments with adult life.

Shackleton did give some clues as to how he was coping, as when he wrote to Petrides from Chile on 7 January 1892: "it is a great pity the way sailors spend their money; in making themselves lower than the very beasts. It is a hard job to keep straight here but I know where to go for help; so I am kept through the many temptations around me."[8] Shackleton was a religious boy and the "help" that he turned to was his Bible and poetry. He even attempted to convince the sailors to sign the pledge of temperance.

Thomas Peers, a shipmate, later told how when Shackleton "wasn't on duty on the deck he was stowed away in his cabin with his books... he was full of it... he could quote poetry."[9] Peers did not elucidate which poets Shackleton was focusing on, but we do know that at home Tennyson was a family favourite. Tennyson's works contain many improving sentiments so one can imagine that, as he sought to keep himself from falling into the bad habits of sailors in port, he may have kept in mind words such as these from Tennyson's "Sir Galahad" (1842):

> My strength is as the strength of ten,
> Because my heart is pure.

Among his books on board, Shackleton had a copy of Edmund Burke's *A Philosophical Enquiry into the Origin of Our Ideas of the Sublime and Beautiful*, written when Burke* was a similar age. Beauty certainly made an impression on Shackleton. Emily later wrote "that his communion with the stars when alone on watch in the clear nights at sea so impressed his mind with the austere purity of Nature, that he could find no attraction in the doubtful haunts of foreign ports; the thought of the stars barred the way." All of this study, avoidance of the fleshpots and nascent bookishness seem to sit at odds with the dashing, party-loving raconteur that Shackleton became in later life.

During these early years Shackleton was teetotal although this did not last far into his exploring years. A verse by George Ade (1866-1944) extolling temperance had lodged in his head and in an article that Shackleton wrote for the *Daily Mail* in 1914 about Christmas Day in Antarctica, he borrowed the last two lines of this verse:

---

* There is a family connection here too, for Edmund Burke was a pupil at Ernest's great-great-great grandfather Abraham Shackleton's famous school in County Kildare.

But R-e-m-o-r-s-e!
The water wagon is the place for me;
It is no time for mirth and laughter,
The cold, gray dawn of the morning after!

*

As Shackleton noted in his talk to the Poetry Society in 1911, he recognized that poetry and exploration were good bedfellows and that poetry had the power to teach. When he read poetry, it was as much to learn from it as for aesthetic pleasure and appreciation.

One of his favourite poets was Rudyard Kipling and, as a young sailor working on ships engaged in troop movements, he would certainly have been familiar with Kipling's poem "A Soldier an' Sailor too". The poem tells a story which could not fail to impress a young merchant seaman and provides a useful illustration of the world of brave ideals, duty and self-control in which he had been brought up. Echoes of the selfless stoicism evoked here would later be heard in Antarctica.

The troop carrier *Birkenhead* sank on the night of 26 February 1852 off Danger Point, South Africa with the loss of two-thirds of those onboard. Many Marines (known as Jollies) and their families were on board when she struck a reef and was holed. Women and children quickly filled the few lifeboats available. The Captain, Robert Salmond, ordered the ship to be abandoned but the officer commanding the troops feared that they would swamp the lifeboats. He ordered the men to remain in their ranks, standing to attention on deck.

So the men stood. The order had been given and was obeyed unquestioningly. Captain Wright, one of the few who survived wrote: "The order and regularity that prevailed on board... far exceeded anything that I thought could be affected by the best discipline... Everyone did as he was directed and there was not a murmur or cry among them..."[10]

Here is verse five of Kipling's six-verse "A Soldier an' Sailor too":

To take your chance in the thick of a rush, with firing all about,
Is nothing so bad when you've cover to 'and, an' leave an' likin' to shout;
But to stand an' be still to the Birken'ead drill is a damn tough bullet
to chew,
An' they done it, the Jollies - 'Er Majesty's Jollies - soldier an' sailor too!
Their work was done when it 'adn't begun; they was younger nor
me an' you;
Their choice it was plain between drownin' in 'eaps an' bein'
mopped by the screw.
So they stood an' was still to the Birken'ead drill, soldier an' sailor too!

Despite Tennyson's assertion that "the path of duty was the way to glory", the stoicism and bravery demonstrated by the *Birkenhead's* men were not enough alone to make an Antarctic Hero. Even as a young man, Shackleton was beginning to show that he was a many sided character capable of leading men through the toughest of times. One shipmate wrote in 1899 that "he was several types bound in one volume."[11] Shackleton described himself as "a curious mixture with something feminine in me as well as being a man."[12] He had identified within himself the more sensitive qualities of empathy and creativity which at the time were considered predominantly female traits.

Nevertheless, the appreciation of poetry was certainly enjoyed by men and women alike, and Shackleton grew up in an era where a cultured life was becoming more attainable. Following the Industrial Revolution, patterns of life were changing. Education and free time were becoming available to all classes of society, and concurrently artistic and literary output was increasing. During Shackleton's childhood, the Football Association was formed, Gilbert joined Sullivan and the six-day working week ended. Census returns for the twenty years between 1891and 1911 show a sharp increase in the number of professional authors, actors, journalists and editors.*

---

* Shackleton would later be among them, as for three months in 1903 he was a sub-editor at *The Royal Magazine*.

As far as poetry was concerned, the Romantic era which began in the mid-eighteenth century had developed as a diametric opposite of preceding Enlightenment ideals. Whereas the latter period's philosophy was largely grounded in concepts of scientific rigour and reason, the Romantics focused on themes of nature, emotion and personal artistic intent. Wordsworth was a leading Romantic, choosing intuition over reason, and through the Industrial Revolution seeking pastoral themes rather than modern and urban motifs. He said that poetry should be "the spontaneous overflow of powerful feelings" coupled with sensibility and thought. Shackleton would be drawn towards these poets of emotion over the next few years and then to neo-Romantics, especially Browning, in whose poems love was entwined with a realistic, hard edge.

It was Shackleton's good fortune to be starting his adult life at a time when there was an increase in cultural production and artistic endeavour combined with sufficient national idealism and technological progress to encourage exploration for the sake of exploring.

∗

The earliest poem from Shackleton's pen to survive is from this early seafaring period of his life. He wrote "A Tale of the Sea" in 1896. He had spent the whole of that year at sea, with only one six-week gap ashore, during which he passed his chief mate examination.

These seven verses recount a dream which features ancient explorers returning honour-laden from travels in the Arctic. The poem compares the ne'er-do-well sailors with whom Shackleton was currently working on the tramp steamer with the explorer sailors whom he described:

As worthy the brightest idyll,
That poet could ever pen.

In an interview in 1910 Shackleton stated that "the circumstance which actually determined me to become an explorer was a dream I had when I was twenty-two" in which he found himself drawn northwards, "to the region of ice and snow and go on and on until I came to one of the poles of the earth."[13] That dream was the inspiration for "A Tale of the Sea":

I slept and dreamt of the ocean:
Of tarry sailors joys:
Of the tales which they loved to fashion
Of days when they were boys:
And I laughed aloud in my sleep:
"In those days they said they were men:
Is there one who has a record
Of worth: for a poets pen"?

The dream soon faded and left me:
But it returned again
And I smelt the Galleys odour
Heard the curses of sailor men.
Heard moaning of bitter salt winds:
Shrieking of gathering gales:
Wings of wild sea birds rising,
Beat the waves like threshers flails.

Then I saw a great long line
Of ghostly ships from the North;
Come churning the seas to foam
Splashing their bows with froth.
Dipping now into the hollows:
Now on the top of they rise;
Pointing their booms to the oceans bed
And anon to the wind swept skies.

They in the foremost ships,
With tattered sails, and torn,
This spoke from the high poop aft:

Where the deck with their tread was worn:
Where nailed to the rotting flagstaffs:
The old white Ensigns flew
Badge of our English freedom
Over all waters blue.

"We fell for our countrys glory
And not for the yellow gold:
No: not as reward for greed:
Has the Arctic o'er us rolled:
We fell for the light of science,
To make clear the hidden paths
When the iceberg crunches our timbers,
As though they were only laths."

Then they told me a wondrous tale
And I strove to write it down
But my pen refused its duty:
And I lost my chance for renown
But since that vision left me:
I have looked on those sailor men
As worthy the brightest idyll,
That poet could ever pen.

Oh! the deepest blue of the sky:
Oh! the greenest sward on the lea:
To me seems dull and paltry,
Since I dreamt of that tossing sea,
For now I know it is peopled
With wandering souls of the past:
Blown to and fro on its surface
At the mercy of every blast.

So Shackleton turned to exploring, inspired by a dream in which he was a poet. For him the roles of explorer and poet were inextricably linked, and he could not be one without the other. Yet he was not just a dreamer. He identified the sea as his school; this is where he grew up, among the tough sailors. He was not afraid of hard work in the real world to realize his dreams.

"A Tale of the Sea" seems to be a condensed synthesis of the influences exerted on Shackleton at that time and a signpost towards his future of exploration "for our country's glory" and the "light of science"—a future when he would "make clear the hidden paths". Dreams, of course, are convenient devices in which to package ambition, for it would have been rather crude for Shackleton to confess that he was taking up exploration in order to make a name for himself, even if it is perhaps closer to the truth.

The first publication of "A Tale of the Sea" was in *The Brisbane Courier* on 26 February 1927. The author of the accompanying article, S. F. A. Coles, asserts that Shackleton wrote the lines "following a chance meeting in early 1895 with a Norwegian whaler called *Antarctic*, just returned from having landed on Antarctica, the first to do so since Ross in 1843". The ship *Antarctic* was not in fact a whaler but a sealing ship, one of its company being Carsten Borchgrevink, who later went on to lead the first party to winter on Antarctica (1899-1900). Although such a meeting in some Australasian port might well have been possible, Shackleton makes no mention of it.

Shackleton wrote a number of his own poems, all of which were composed when he was at sea or on expedition. Their appeal was originally limited to the audience for whom they were produced; his family at home and later colleagues on expeditions. This was due to the subject matter and the relatively low literary worth of his output, which family and friends are naturally willing to overlook.

Other than in the amateur newspapers later produced by and for the men of the expeditions, Shackleton had no thoughts of publishing his poetry for public consumption. One or two verses appeared in *Life* magazine shortly after his death, prompting one Thomas German-Reed to write to Heinemann, Shackleton's publishers, to enquire if a volume of Shackleton's poems might be published. Lady Shackleton concluded that "I don't think there are enough 'poems' to make it worth while even if they were literary enough."[14] As a former student of poetry following the

University Extension Scheme, Emily realized that while they do provide us with access to the mind of the man, his verses were not of sufficient quality or quantity to stand alone. In terms of Shackleton's poetic ability, "his reach exceeded his grasp".

He was serving on the clipper *Hoghton Tower* when he wrote "A Tale of the Sea", on a long voyage that took in much of the southern hemisphere over a fourteen-month period. His focus at that time was not on exploration but promotion. Having started on the lowest rung, Shackleton had risen slowly through the ranks. "My father thought to cure me of my predilection for the sea by letting me go in the most primitive manner possible as a 'boy' on board a sailing ship,"[15] but the remedy was not effective and Shackleton spent ten years at sea in the merchant navy.

During those ten years, he rounded the Horn, carried cargoes to the Far East, troops to South Africa and passed his Master's examination. This put him on the top rung, able to command any British merchant ship. His returns home were infrequent and brief. It was on one such leave period of just eighteen days, sandwiched between four-month and seven-month tours at sea, that he met a woman who was to have an important influence on both his poetic tastes and his exploring life: Emily Dorman.

3 EMILY

There is a myth attached to Shackleton's first meeting with Emily Dorman. Apparently she was attracted to a strong-looking young man who had a copy of Robert Browning's works sticking out of his pocket. Emily later set the record straight: "When I first knew Ernest I was steeped in R.B. and I remember most distinctly, his saying he did not care for him." His introduction to Browning came from Emily; she started him gently with a gift for his birthday in 1898 of an edition of the *Pocket Volume of Selections from the Poetical Works of Robert Browning*. "Ernest loved Browning from that time onwards," she wrote, and he even took a slim Browning volume with him on his journey towards the South Pole in 1907-9.

From that first exchange, poetry became a theme of their letters and discussions. Where Shackleton's own pen failed him, he would borrow from others, sending in his earliest extant letter

Ernest and Emily Shackleton in later life
(Library of Congress, Washington DC)

to Emily a Browning verse: not a Robert, but Elizabeth Barrett Browning's famous "Sonnet 43". Of their courtship Emily said, "He had such a strong attraction for me, and we had books, poetry and small literary aspirations in common."[16]

Sonnet 43

How do I love thee? Let me count the ways.
I love thee to the depth and breadth and height
My soul can reach, when feeling out of sight
For the ends of being and ideal grace.
I love thee to the level of everyday's
Most quiet need, by sun and candlelight.
I love thee freely, as men strive for right;
I love thee purely, as they turn from praise.
I love thee with a passion put to use
In my old griefs, and with my childhood's faith.
I love thee with a love I seemed to lose
With my lost saints, —I love thee with the breath,
Smiles, tears, of all my life! —and, if God choose,
I shall but love thee better after death.

Clearly love-struck, Ernest wrote that every night he looked at "our star". Emily does not comment directly on her level of attraction towards him as it was apparently not strong in the initial stages of the relationship. She felt she was "not worthy of such love". Emily was also worried about her age since she was six years older than Shackleton. This was also a factor for Elizabeth Barrett Browning, but Ernest sought to reassure Emily, writing, "And when [Elizabeth] married she was 37 years old that was not too old for 15 years of bliss and life and he was three years younger than she..."[17] Emily would be 36 when she wed, and the Shackletons enjoyed seventeen years of marriage.

Throughout their marriage it seemed as though the Shackletons leaned on the Brownings for an unorthodox form of marriage guidance. Neither couple had a conventional marriage or working life, but both were able to enjoy love and happiness despite facing difficulties. For the Brownings the main problem was Elizabeth's constant ill health, while for the Shackletons the source of trouble was Ernest's absences and infidelities. The Brownings became an example for the Shackletons to aspire to: "How happy that woman must have been who wrote these lines."[18]

✳

Both Emily and Ernest grew up in large, sociable families. Emily Dorman, born in 1868, had five siblings. The Dormans lived comfortably thanks to her father Charles' legal business in London and family farm in Kent. For Ernest, the primary benefit of having eight sisters was to be able to meet their many girlfriends. Ethel Shackleton recalled that her brother wrote "more interesting letters & fuller than ever before" after meeting her new friend, Emily Dorman. Ernest's interest was piqued by this challenging, confident, older woman. "He described sunsets and quoted poetry," Ethel continued, "and on a tiny scrap of paper he wrote 'I don't mind if you do show my letter to your friend'."[19]

Ernest had first met Emily when he was 23 and she 29, at a house party at her home, in 1897. He then returned to sea aboard *Flintshire* and initially communicated with Emily through Ethel. Ethel was disappointed that these lovely letters were not being written for her benefit alone. Shackleton, meanwhile, was keen to gauge Emily's reaction. He asked Ethel, "Be sure to say when you write [back] what notice she took."[20] When his ship ran aground off Middlesbrough at New Year 1898, he was granted 24 hours leave, ostensibly to visit his father for his birthday, but naturally he stopped off to see Miss Dorman.

Emily recalled him declaring his love for her at this meeting and she clearly remembered that "he put his cigarette on a ledge in the big oak chimney piece"; alas, the pair were so intent on one another that the glowing cigarette was forgotten about and "it burnt a deep dent."[21] Emily wanted to retain that mantelpiece as a keepsake, but she regretted that she would never have a house large enough in which to mount it.

We have a lot to thank Emily Dorman for. It was she who introduced Ernest to Robert Browning and fostered, through discussion and correspondence, his love of other poets too. In that first letter, writing home from Port Said on 12 August 1898, Ernest seemed to be replying to a question from Emily: "The moral of the 'Statue and the Bust'. Surely you know; it is plain [and] true... to me! 'That a man should strive to the uttermost for his life's set prize'."

This misquotation of a line by Browning was one of the poetic phrases which became part of Shackleton's unique creed although his "life's set prize" was not just Emily. For as much as she was a hard-won prize, once attained Shackleton would need to strive again for the next goal.

*

Emily was the recipient and collector of a large body of letters written by Shackleton throughout his life. Few of her letters to him survive and letters from before their marriage have for the most part been lost. In searching for clues as to the foundations and development of Ernest and Emily's relationship and the poems that brought them together, we have to fast-forward to Emily's reminiscences prepared for Shackleton's first serious biographer.[*]

Emily began the journey to an approved biography by approaching a potential author, Hugh Robert Mill. Mill was a geographer, historian and, crucially for Emily, he had known Shackleton, having sailed with him on *Discovery*, but he had left the ship before she reached Antarctica. Over eleven months Emily and Mill collaborated, mostly by letter, to produce *The Life of Sir Ernest Shackleton*. This volume, when read with the letters, becomes "The Life of Emily and Ernest Shackleton". The

---

[*] An unauthorized "biography" by Harold Begbie was rushed into print shortly after Shackleton's death, by the Mills & Boon company. Normally associated with romantic novels, the publishers sought to cash in on the explorer's death with this lightly written, slim volume.

biography is by today's standards too reverential to Shackleton's memory and omits many of the personal details of his life. Mill prefers to concentrate on the voyages of exploration and relationships surrounding them.

For Emily, the process of sorting through the letters and documents cannot have been easy. Shackleton had died just four months previously. "I must go steadily through the letters he wrote to me, also, but it makes me cry."[22] Later, she described the exercise as "a balm". One of the first packets of letters that she sent to Mill includes two of Shackleton's own poems, written while he was on his first expedition to Antarctica, "The Great Barrier" and "L'Envoi". After signing off this brief note she adds, "the verses have taken me 'down South' and I have not got back yet." Emily and Ernest had such a strong, if elastic, marriage bond that his own simple lines were able to reach out to her, from a grave 8,000 miles away.

Mill was a sound choice for a biographer. Though a friend of the Shackletons, he sought wherever possible to present a balanced picture. He admitted early on that "one can not show the springs of Ernest's character without bringing in [Emily's] influence on him".

Shackleton's start in exploration coincided with the start of his relationship with Emily; Mill understood that to study Ernest we need to know Emily too. "Lady Shackleton... was... mainly responsible... in raising him from a rather dreamy ambitious boy with no settled ideas into a man of strong character,"[23] wrote Albert Armitage, a man who sailed with Shackleton (and Mill, initially) on *Discovery*.

Emily was instrumental in suggesting poetic quotations with which to head, and epitomize, each chapter of Ernest's life in the biography. These epigraphs are a mixture of Browning, Robert Service, Matthew Arnold and Tennyson. They all share the common theme of knightly purpose or some honourable goal to which men should strive. None mentions love, home life or satisfaction.

Would Emily have continued her relationship with Shackleton had she known that his striving nature would lead him to a life of restless adventuring and cause her such unhappiness? Such thoughts were not in her mind as she recounted their early courtship to Mill: "I must send you the little book we shared in 1898. It is part of my heart." This was a notebook into which each would write favourite poetic quotations as "literature [was] opening out wonderful vistas". As a couple they were embarking on a shared expedition into poetry. It was a cherished memory for Emily: "I often longed to recapture those early days, but there was never time—and he was doing bigger things and making his own bit of History after all."[24]

Emily had a head start on Ernest when it came to the study of poetry. Since 1870, University Extension schemes had been created by the Universities of Oxford, Cambridge and London. These open-access lecture series were held over twelve weeks' duration and taught by university lecturers in various provincial and suburban locations. Before her marriage, Emily had attended such a course under the tutelage of Churton Collins. He was a self-taught critic of English literature and a Professor at the University of Birmingham. Emily submitted papers on subjects including Browning's poems "Paracelsus" and "The Ring and the Book". She took full part in the course, relishing the challenge of homework and submitting work to academic critique.

It was to Browning's "Paracelsus" that Shackleton turned when inspiration deserted him as he tried to explain his attitude towards married life to Emily in 1898. "Paracelsus" is a long, difficult poem; the eponymous hero, a Swiss-German Renaissance physician and alchemist,* puts aside love in order to seek knowledge. The poem marked a clear break with the preceding Romantic period where love conquered all, and Browning's neo-Romantic outlook has a less idealistic and more pragmatic edge. Paracelsus

---

* Paracelsus was born Philippus Aureolus Theophrastus Bombastus von Hohenheim in 1493. In both the poem and real life, he lived up to his middle name with a bombastic, supremely self-confident style.

chooses enlightenment over love and inevitably falls from favour as a result. His ambition uncompromised, Paracelsus realizes too late that although he has gained the knowledge that he desires, he is incomplete, and turns to grosser pleasures before, in old age, settling his mind with thoughts that, whilst he has made a mistake, it is too late to rectify.

This was a notion that Shackleton rejected "I do not want Paracelsus's happiness," he wrote. "What I call success[:] a few years praise from those around and then down to the grave with the best thing missed;..."[25] He rejected the visible path ahead to career success as a ship's captain, even though he did not yet know of the other path to success through exploration. He wanted to have it all: success in time (though "for me it seems a long way off," he wrote in the same letter) and the love of Emily*.

At times, Shackleton, like Paracelsus, could be bombastic; certainly those men who were not "with" him would have seen more of this side of his nature. This was still some years ahead: it would take the challenge of forming and maintaining a relationship with Emily to bring out such confidence in him. Emily acknowledged that "my father liked him... [but] there were others who thought the friendship foolish". A young sailor with little education and no visible prospects beyond that of making the rank of captain—it is easy to see why some of her friends might have thought this was not the most suitable union.

Shackleton was setting his sights high but had seen in the press the increasing activity and interest surrounding Antarctica. The conquest of the Pole would be a worthy prize to lay at Emily's feet, and so he applied to join the British National Antarctic Expedition. After six months of waiting—and with a reference that read "His brother officers considered him to be a very

---

* Love and success in the Polar Regions do not necessarily sit well together. Of Shackleton's contemporaries, Roald Amundsen never married, De Gerlache married twice and Charcot was divorced by his wife after his first Antarctic expedition on the grounds of desertion!

EFFIGIES PARASELCI MEDICI CELEBERRIMI

Etching of Paracelsus by Wenceslaus Hollar (1607-1677)
(Wikimedia Commons)

good fellow, always quoting poetry and full of erratic ideas,"[26]—Shackleton was accepted onto a path that he would follow for the rest of his life.

As he told a shipmate, he was going south "for her."[27] This was not just to impress her but in order to establish a reputation for himself and therefore gain the financial reward that would make him feel more worthy of her hand. He wrote to Emily's father, Charles Dorman: "…it is mainly for one reason that I am going, is to get on so that when I come back or later when I have made money I might with your permission marry Emily…"[28] Dorman replied that if when Ernest returned, Emily still wanted to, his consent would be forthcoming. The caveat was inserted because Ernest by this time was on board *Discovery* and would not be home for two years. Shackleton became a member of the expedition sight-unseen, based on the recommendations of previous captains and employers. Shackleton also had a friendship with Cedric Longstaff, the son of a major sponsor of the expedition, and no doubt this personal connection helped with his appointment. He was being set free from the drudgery of ships on regular passages; he saw a gleaming, untravelled world ahead.

4 NEMO JOINS *DISCOVERY*

When Shackleton signed up for the National Antarctic Expedition in 1901 he hoped to make the journey from an unknown merchant seaman to a man of action; he wrote: "... my future is all to make but I intend making it quickly."[29] The expedition departed on RRS *Discovery* after a royal send off from Cowes Week in 1901 with the aim of securing the South Pole for the Empire. Shackleton's aim was altogether more personal.

Like many visitors to Antarctica, he found it difficult to put his first impressions of the region into words. This is partly because, as he confided in his diary, he was feeling homesick. He altered a Browning poem title when he wrote that he was having "home thoughts from the ice."[30] "Home Thoughts from Abroad" eulogizes springtime in England and is more likely to have enhanced homesickness rather than alleviated it.

RRS *Discovery* at her home port of Dundee
(Julian Nitzche/Wikimedia Commons)

Home Thoughts from Abroad

O, To be in England
Now that April's there,
And whoever wakes in England
Sees, some morning, unaware,
That the lowest boughs and the brushwood sheaf
Round the elm-tree bole are in tiny leaf,
While the chaffinch sings on the orchard bough
In England—now!

And after April, when May follows,
And the whitethroat builds, and all the swallows!
Hark, where my blossom'd pear-tree in the hedge
Leans to the field and scatters on the clover
Blossoms and dewdrops—at the bent spray's edge—
That's the wise thrush; he sings each song twice over,
Lest you should think he never could recapture
The first fine careless rapture!
And though the fields look rough with hoary dew,
All will be gay when noontide wakes anew
The buttercups, the little children's dower
—Far brighter than this gaudy melon-flower!

Robert Browning also provided a reference for the "unique sort of feeling to look on lands that have never been seen by human eye before."[31] There was little information to prepare the team for what they would see. The only previous expedition to have been close, Borchgrevink's in 1899-1900, brought home a handful of grainy black and white photographs. This scarcity of information and images is hard for us to comprehend today as from our desks we can instantly call up pictures of any corner of the globe. Shackleton described the area around their winter quarters as having a "weird and uncanny look, and reminded me of the desert in 'Childe Rowland to the Dark Tower Came'."[32]

He had chosen his reference well. The poem is enigmatic, depicting a landscape that is strange, deformed, challenging the imagination. The figures in the poem are silent: as the men onboard *Discovery* might have been rendered dumb by the beauty of Antarctica as they manned the rail and stared out. For a physical encapsulation of snow-free moraine, "Bog, clay, and rubble, sand and stark black dearth" serves well. "No sound, no sight as far as eye could strain" captures the scene's wide emptiness. Yet the poem, like Antarctica, is a "compound of legend and fairytale, mysticism and dream."[33] It contains more than a physical description, capturing also the emotion of looking on these wonders for the first time. The poem also creates the idea of a chivalric quest, fitting for the southward march to come. Self-doubt, created by his homesickness, might have crept into Shackleton's mind:

> The knights who to the Dark Tower's search addressed,
> Their steps—that just to fail as they, seemed best,
> And all the doubt was now—should I be fit?

Most Browning poems have characters at their core, but in this piece it is the landscape that takes centre stage. The crew of *Discovery* would have felt the same emotions as they arrived in Antarctica: suddenly the landscape dominated. All the hazards encountered, decisions to be made and forces acting on the ship came from the poorly understood and spectacular geography that then surrounded them. The quest of Browning's knight over a barren plain to a mysterious tower merges with the southern sledge journey over white snow to come.

> …grey plain all round:
> Nothing but plain to the horizon's bound.
> I might go on; nought else remained to do.

In Browning's poem there seems to be no reward once the Dark Tower is reached and so too at the Pole; here, the only thing for explorers to do is turn back and retrace their ski tracks to the north. Indeed, it is hard to know when one is at the South Pole: there is no visible or tangible "pole" and the landscape is the same for miles around. The knight does not know when he is at the tower:

> Burningly it came on me all at once,
> This was the place! those two hills on the right,
> Crouched like two bulls locked horn in horn in fight;
> While to the left, a tall scalped mountain... Dunce,
> Dotard, a-dozing at the very nonce,
> After a life spent training for the sight!

This southern quest is in the future; Shackleton, Scott and rest of *Discovery*'s crew first had to settle in and prepare for the winter.

*

They wintered at what they named Hut Point on the south side of Ross Island and, once *Discovery* was iced in, she was transformed from a sailing vessel into an Antarctic base. One of Shackleton's tasks prior to departure, as he obtained and stowed essential provisions and equipment, had been to procure wigs and dresses for the planned theatricals. These entertainments were a feature of British polar winters from the early Victorian forays into the Arctic and continue to the present day.

As a further winter distraction for the men "...it was decided to bring out a monthly paper... Shackleton was appointed editor."[34] It was a task to which he was perfectly suited and, as Edward Wilson noted in his diary, "the [only] typewriter was his possession". *The South Polar Times* was a magazine volume, produced every few weeks by and for the members of the expedition. Editions contained a variety of stories, factual reports, pictures and poems. Shackleton wrote in his first editorial that the magazine was both "grave and gay". Only one copy of each edition would be produced, carefully bound in thin wooden boards, with some editions also sporting a seal-skin covering. Richly illustrated with Wilson's paintings, each volume was a work of art.

Shackleton's appointment appears to have come about by

universal acclamation from the members of the ward room. Had he seen this coming, Scott may have been inclined to pre-empt the appointment and select another for the post, not because it was Shackleton who was chosen but because of the influence that such a magazine could have on the rest of the expedition members. The choice of Shackleton, coming from his fellow officers, was a special form of promotion for the third officer,

THE SOUTH POLAR TIMES 41

they sleep in the winter, and for how many hours a day, is a problem full of interest. Now and again as we walk among the Weddell's Seals we find a Crab-eater, seldom more than one or two, asleep with the rest.

When we were in the pack ice these were our daily food, for we saw some every day, and often ate them. Here they are a rarity, and an interesting one, as they have hitherto been considered the peculiar property of the pack ice. The "Southern Cross" expedition found one on the Great Ice Barrier, and we saw several as we sailed along it, but here we have them still farther South, and prospect of our from time to

there seems every seeing them time during the winter and perhaps even some--thing of their family arrangements in the Spring. I think the general admiration of our party is divided somewhat between the Crab-eater and Ross' Seal. We have had but few opportunities of getting to know the latter, though both are very interesting. No one has ever met with Ross' Seal except in the pack ice, and possibly his coat would be found to vary much if seen at other seasons of the year, but he has only been seen in summer when all have had a roughish hair

Sea Leopard chasing Emperor Penguins

The South Polar Times, edited by Shackleton, illustrated by Wilson (private collection)

31

and an example of what biographer Roland Huntford described as Shackleton's "psychological leadership" of the wintering party.[35] Now Shackleton had an official outlet for his talents. The editorial direction of *The South Polar Times* was entirely up to him: Captain Scott only saw the edition once it was complete, just a few hours before it was released to the rest of the ship's company.

Shackleton set up a small office for himself and Wilson down in the hold among the packing cases of chocolate and raisins, which they would "keep an eye on to see that they don't get spoilt by the damp."[36] Albert Armitage, second in command of *Discovery*, noted that Shackleton had moved his office to the hold "in self-defence" so that his "poetic nerves could be at rest". Shackleton had brought with him from the merchant marine a reputation as a book-loving poet. While he certainly would have enjoyed a measure of quiet in which to write, he actually thrived on company and conversation. During this winter period, closeted in a snug office with Wilson, their friendship grew; appellations were shortened to Shackles and Billy. Like two schoolboys they got up to literary mischief while hidden among the tuck.

Controlling entry to this den with a piece of string attached to the door handle, Shackleton encouraged contributions from the lower decks and would have been visited by men who recognized that their contributions required a little informal editing. He got to know more of the men and learnt the importance of building relationships with the sailors, a lesson that was to be so useful to him in his future expeditions.

Shackleton wrote the editorial, commending the first edition to his readers. When he wrote prose, it became a rendering in print of his own voice. His choice of words and metre is ready for speech. Throughout his life he found live conversations, lectures and meetings easier than the written word. As a result, it is often better to hear Shackleton's phrasing than to read it. The original readers of *The South Polar Times*, on board *Discovery*, had an advantage over later readers because they were familiar with

Shackleton's voice. It became traditional that Scott, seated at the head of the table, would read aloud from the paper on the first day of its publication. Afterwards each monthly issue would then be passed around for everyone to enjoy.

Shackleton could not help but slip a (slightly adjusted) line from Tennyson's "Ulysses" into the first edition. He compared his cohort with "those men of old, who ever with a frolic welcome took the storm and sunshine". All of his fellow officers would have recognized this allusion. (Shackleton substituted "storm" for the original "thunder", knowing that it is impossible to have a thunderstorm in Antarctica because there is insufficient temperature difference between the cool near-surface air and the higher air mass in the clouds.)

Tennyson's poems were a feature of the *Discovery* story. They cropped up in another form of winter entertainment: a series of debates. These often lively affairs were for the amusement of the scientists and officers more than for the men. Shackleton took full part and one evening the subject was Browning vs. Tennyson: who was the better poet? Shackleton put the case for Browning and, with his detailed knowledge of both poets and his persuasive Irish rhetoric, ought to have been able to swing the house to his side of the argument, but it was not to be. Louis Bernacchi (who, despite his name, was an Australian) championed Tennyson and won, but by only one vote.

*

For his own poetic contributions to *The South Polar Times*, Shackleton chose to use the pseudonym Nemo. In an earlier letter to Emily he wrote "my name is Nemo"[37] as he lamented his poverty and lack of career prospects. Latin for no-one, it summed up who he thought he was at that time.

Captain Nemo, the hero of Jules Verne's *Twenty Thousand Leagues under the Sea*, displayed an exploring spirit and unique character which Shackleton would have admired. Captain

Nemo's submarine, *Nautilus*, even made it as far the Antarctic. When the narrator, Professor Aronnax, asks of Nemo "In these polar seas forbidden to man, did he not feel right at home, the lord of these unreachable regions?" he may well have been asking it of Shackleton. Although Shackleton's primary motivation in venturing south was to make a name for himself (he would have canoed up the Nile if he thought it would help) he clearly fell in love with Antarctica and his subsequent returns were as much for his love of the icy continent as they were for striving for gain.

It was the grandest Antarctic vistas that captured Shackleton's imagination and became the subjects of his own poetic contributions, first "To the Great Barrier" and later "Midwinter's Night" and "Erebus". Clearly under Tennyson's powerful influence, Shackleton invoked kings, winds from all cardinal points and images of guarded, secure territories. Several times he reminds the reader that just to look upon these lands is a physical and psychological strain; how much more effort would it be to travel over them?

The Great Ice Barrier (now known as the Ross Ice Shelf) is a plain of ice about the size of France. At its northern boundary the Barrier meets the sea in a cliff wall almost 170 feet high and is over 300 miles wide. The southern edge is attached to the Antarctic continent. Fed by glaciers flowing down from the polar plateau, the whole mass slowly moves north as a conveyor-belt of ice, calving huge tabular icebergs into the sea at the end of the process. This feature was discovered by James Clark Ross in 1841 and is now named after him. Sailing south through the Ross Sea towards the Barrier, vessels were able to penetrate further south by sea than at any other point around the Antarctic coast. All would then be brought up short by this impassable wall of ice.

Although the Barrier closed the way for further sailing, once the ice cliff was scaled the gently sloping surface of the Barrier provided the obvious route south for overland travel. Yet it had remained untouched by human foot until just a year before *Discovery* sailed south. In 1900 Carsten Borchgrevink had made a short journey over the Barrier but it still remained a mystery. The men climbed the ship's rigging and coastal mountains attempting to peer south but still, until the sledging season came, the questions of the poem remained unanswered. There is a hint of Swinburne too, in the opening lines of "To the Great Barrier". "Mother of mighty icebergs" is reminiscent of

> ...the great sweet mother,
> Mother and lover of men, the sea...

from Swinburne's "The Triumph of Time".

There is the feeling of a knightly quest about this poem and perhaps the pen name Nemo was also adopted in recognition that however noble or knightly the explorers felt as they left home, they were nobodies when set against the vastness of unexplored Antarctica. Their challenge was huge. We now know so much about all corners of the earth that it is difficult to comprehend to what extent these early expeditions were stepping into *terra incognita*. Shackleton wrote: "We have felt, more than seen, the danger." They could not yet imagine the nature and shape of the hazards they were to face. They were able to sense the danger to the south but struggled to name or identify it.

In "To the Great Barrier", Shackleton listed the expedition's accomplishments so far: sailing east and west along the Great Ice Barrier, from volcanic Mount Erebus in the west to an ice-clogged sea in the east; sounding the depths in the barely charted seas as they went. Then we read the line, "We have risen above your surface", which we can take in the literal sense. Their flight was not one of imagination but in a hydrogen-filled cow-gut balloon, funding for which had been secured by Shackleton. Scott ascended first but the second tethered flight was taken by Shackleton. He made sure to go a little higher than Scott but also took useful photographs of the south, where all that he could see was the "league upon league of whiteness" waiting to be traversed the following season.

To the Great Barrier

Mother of mighty icebergs, these Kings of the Southern Seas,
Mystery, yet unfathomed, though we've paid in full our fees,
Eyes strained by ceaseless watching, when the low grey fog doth screen
Your walls from our aching vision, and the great grim giants you wean
Away from your broad white bosom, where for aeons untold is laid
Each yearly tribute of fallen snows, that this wonderful plain has made.
We have felt, more than seen, the danger, close ahead of our long jib boom,
But a turn of the icy wheel has made for us more sea room.
We have sailed from your farthest West, that is bounded by fire and snow,
We have pierced to your farthest East, till stopped by the hard, set floe.
We have steamed by your wave worn caverns; dim, blue, mysterious halls,
We have risen above your surface, we have sounded along your walls.
And above that rolling surface we have strained our eyes to see,
But league upon league of whiteness was all that there seemed to be.
Ah, what is the secret you're keeping, to the Southward beyond our ken?
This year shall your icy fastness resound with the voices of men?
Shall we learn that you come from the mountains? Shall we call you a
frozen sea?
Shall we sail to the Northward and leave you, still a Secret for ever to be?

Nemo, *The South Polar Times*, August 1902

"To the Great Barrier" sets out the task of adventure ahead of
the explorers, as they settled in for the winter. This was the
honeymoon time for the expedition, relationships were new
and fresh, the oncoming winter a novelty. It was the only poem
of Shackleton's to be published in *The South Polar Times* while
he was on the expedition. I wonder whether editorial scruples
prevented him from including more of his own works.

5 ULYSSES RETURNS

Having distinguished himself during the early part of the expedition and preparatory sledge journeys, Shackleton was selected for the journey towards the South Pole which commenced on 2 November 1902. By 15 November, the supporting parties had turned back and left Scott, Wilson and Shackleton to continue on their own. Louis Bernacchi described the scene: "The three polar knights... they were away... with banners flying in the wind." Each man had his own sledging flag, redolent of the heraldic devices on a knight's shield or tunic. The flags were Sir Clements Markham's idea, continuing the familiar portrayal of polar expeditions in contemporary literature as "a testing ground for upper class Victorian heroic masculinity."[38] Once wrapped up in their gabardine with balaclavas and goggles covering their faces, the three may well have been as unidentifiable as armoured knights, but in this tournament their only foes were the elements, which do not discriminate.

Morale quickly slipped away as, lacking experience of dog driving, they were forced to pull the sledges alongside the dogs. With heavy loads and contending with thick snow they moved each sledge in relays, achieving only four miles of forward progress per day. The team realized that at this rate any hope of attaining the Pole was lost. There was little cheer on the southern journey: it was a slog. Shortly after Christmas, for which Shackleton had produced a tiny pudding that he had kept hidden in a spare sock for the three to share, the decision was made to turn back.

They had pushed beyond the limits of human knowledge and endeavour, and yet 82°15' south was not much of a Furthest South, when the aim of the expedition had been the pole.

At the Pole, at the Pole,
Britannia's pretty sure to reach her goal:
Her ever-conquering legions,
Will annex those distant regions,
And make a new dominion of the Pole.[39]

So *The Referee* newspaper had trumpeted following the announcement that the National Antarctic Expedition would be striving southwards. This, however, was not to be the case, and with the Pole still 420 miles distant and Midsummer's Day already past, the three turned northwards, adding the weight of disappointment to their already heavy sledges.

Although the journey to the Pole proved too ambitious for these first-time polar explorers, we must remember that this expedition was only the third to ever overwinter in Antarctica and was the first to seriously explore the Great Barrier. Somehow, though, despite his disappointment at a goal missed and with waning confidence in his leader, Shackleton remained optimistic. As they turned north he wrote, "it is a wonderful place and deserves the trouble... it takes to get here."[40]

Each of the three men would have had long conversations with his own inner voice as they trudged along. Although physically they were walking close enough to speak to one another, their muffled faces and the effort of pulling prevented much talk. And so each turned inwards to his own mental sanctuary and silent dialogue.

For Scott, this was the loneliest point; he was feeling intense anxiety about the future, for even when surrounded by a team, the leader can find himself alone. Walking for hours towards a blank white horizon and spiritually out of touch with those physically closest to him, Scott mulled over the problems of that day, the days ahead and the future. Darker still, endless "what ifs?" arrived unannounced and uninvited in his mind.

Wilson's mental discourse, reflected in his diaries and letters, was always with The Almighty. His biographer, George Seaver discerned that "though Royds in one way and Scott in another

Captain Robert Falcon Scott, pictured after the *Discovery* expedition (Wikimedia Commons)

came nearest to him in understanding... yet with neither of them could he exchange those ideas on the deep things of life which were always in the background of his mind."[41] Wilson wrote in his diary that "I feel it is all communion with God."[42]

Shackleton turned to poetry during that march northward. "Tennyson's *Ulysses* keeps running through my mind," he wrote.[43] Alfred, Lord Tennyson, was Britain's longest-serving Poet Laureate, from 1850 until his death in 1892. Just five years earlier, Shackleton started at Dulwich College and Tennyson would certainly have been on the curriculum, with poems such as "Ulysses" supporting the study of classical mythology. Tennyson was widely known to all the expedition members, but seems to have been most firmly imprinted in Shackleton's memory. Years later, classical references came automatically to Shackleton's mind as he dictated the book *South*, describing an "icy Cerberus"[44] guarding the lead (an open waterway between ice floes) to safe water.

It is hard to find a more apt poem to encapsulate Shackleton's restlessness, his need to make a name for himself and to complete "some work of noble note". "Ulysses" was not only right for that moment on the Barrier, but for the whole of Shackleton's life. The poem is based on the story of Odysseus who is blown off course, suffers shipwreck and loss, takes lovers and through his ten-year journey is resourceful, inventive and (unlike Paracelsus) ultimately successful. Tennyson described how the King, returned home, was still restless for more adventure and thus determined to see out his final days in some last great odyssey. The end for Shackleton, too, is contained within Tennyson's lines: "to sail beyond the sunset and the baths of all the western stars until I die."

Ulysses

It little profits that an idle king,
By this still hearth, among these barren crags,
Match'd with an aged wife, I mete and dole

Unequal laws unto a savage race,
That hoard, and sleep, and feed, and know not me.
I cannot rest from travel: I will drink
Life to the lees: All times I have enjoy'd
Greatly, have suffer'd greatly, both with those
That loved me, and alone; on shore, and when
Thro' scudding drifts the rainy Hyades
Vext the dim sea: I am become a name;
For always roaming with a hungry heart
Much have I seen and known; cities of men
And manners, climates, councils, governments,
Myself not least, but honour'd of them all;
And drunk delight of battle with my peers,
Far on the ringing plains of windy Troy.
I am a part of all that I have met;
Yet all experience is an arch wherethro'
Gleams that untravell'd world, whose margin fades
For ever and for ever when I move.
How dull it is to pause, to make an end,
To rust unburnish'd, not to shine in use!
As tho' to breathe were life. Life piled on life
Were all too little, and of one to me
Little remains: but every hour is saved
From that eternal silence, something more,
A bringer of new things; and vile it were
For some three suns to store and hoard myself,
And this grey spirit yearning in desire
To follow knowledge like a sinking star,
Beyond the utmost bound of human thought.

This my son, mine own Telemachus,
To whom I leave the sceptre and the isle -
Well-loved of me, discerning to fulfil
This labour, by slow prudence to make mild
A rugged people, and through soft degrees
Subdue them to the useful and the good.
Most blameless is he, centered in the sphere
Of common duties, decent not to fail
In offices of tenderness, and pay
Meet adoration to my household gods,
When I am gone. He works his work, I mine.

There lies the port; the vessel puffs her sail:
There gloom the dark broad seas. My mariners,
Souls that have toiled, and wrought, and thought with me -
That ever with a frolic welcome took
The thunder and the sunshine, and opposed
Free hearts, free foreheads—you and I are old;
Old age hath yet his honour and his toil;
Death closes all: but something ere the end,
Some work of noble note, may yet be done,
Not unbecoming men that strove with Gods.
The lights begin to twinkle from the rocks:
The long day wanes: the slow moon climbs: the deep
Moans round with many voices. Come, my friends,
'Tis not too late to seek a newer world.
Push off, and sitting well in order smite
The sounding furrows; for my purpose holds
To sail beyond the sunset, and the baths
Of all the western stars, until I die.
It may be that the gulfs will wash us down:
It may be we shall touch the Happy Isles,
And see the great Achilles, whom we knew
Tho' much is taken, much abides; and tho'
We are not now that strength which in old days
Moved earth and heaven; that which we are, we are;
One equal temper of heroic hearts,
Made weak by time and fate, but strong in will
To strive, to seek, to find, and not to yield.

Like many boys of his generation, Shackleton would have been attracted to "Ulysses" by the protagonist's heroic desire for the pursuit of knowledge through adventure. Later he would have empathized with the ease with which Ulysses seems able to abandon his wife and son, with whom he has only recently been re-acquainted, in order to set out again and roam with a hungry heart. There is no doubt that Shackleton loved Emily, but he was also happy to be apart from her; he trusted her (as Ulysses trusted Telemachus) to look after his "kingdom" in his absence. It is perhaps interesting to re-read lines of the second part of "Ulysses" substituting Emily for Ulysses' son Telemachus.

Most blameless is [she], centered in the sphere
Of common duties, decent not to fail

*

Despite the hard-going of the return journey and the disappointment of an objective unrealized, all three men gained some satisfaction from the journey. Each of them later returned to the same spot and set out again for the same goal.

...all times I have enjoy'd
Greatly, have suffer'd greatly, both with those
That loved me and alone:

A further suffering was ahead: all three were labouring under the scourge of scurvy.

The disease could be avoided, even if the science behind the remedies was not fully understood until the 1930s. Their sledging rations were deficient in sources of Vitamin C and the lemon juice used at the winter quarters was of inferior quality; thus when the men started out on their sledging expeditions they were already suffering from a lack of antiscorbutics. Wilson, as the doctor in the party, first suspected scurvy on Christmas Eve, 1902. In the week following Shackleton's note about "Ulysses", Wilson observed day after day a gradual deterioration in Shackleton's condition as the scurvy took hold. In addition to the physically debilitating effects of toothache, lethargy and sores, scurvy can make the sufferer depressed. Even for the ever optimistic Shackleton, these were dark days.

Unlike Scott, Shackleton was not predisposed to depression but obviously he suffered during this period of the expedition, as evidenced by his increasingly brief diary entries, which eventually dry up altogether. He was also under the shadow of the heart problems that plagued his whole life. Wilson noted in his diary that such problems "are of no small consequence a hundred and sixty miles from the ship."[45]

Shackleton's own diary made only slight references to being "on the sick list", but the absence of substantial entries tells a tale. It is on Wilson that we must rely for more objective reports on his condition. "Shackleton very poorly indeed all day, very breathless... and quite unfit to move."[46] By this stage he was "made weak by time and fate". On the evidence of Wilson's diary, we can say that Shackleton was certainly "not now that strength which in old days moved earth and heaven." Yet for each of these negative phrases, Tennyson provides Ulysses with a positive rejoinder; he is still "strong in will" and "Though much is taken, much abides." Here too, Shackleton would have drawn strength.

The party had inexplicably thrown away all but one pair of skis, despite Wilson noting that "it is far less fatigue in this snow travelling on ski than on foot."[47] The remaining pair was given to Shackleton and he was forbidden to pull the sledge. The swish-swish rhythm of skis and poles might perhaps have kept time with a mantra from "Ulysses" running through his head—"not to yield, not to yield"—which would have fitted well with his laboured breathing. The party had been out on the march for 74 days, and they still had twenty days to go before the next bath and change of clothes.

Shackleton continued under his own power on skis following along behind Wilson and Scott but unable to contribute to the pulling of the sledge. The trio at this point were not "one equal temper of heroic hearts". Scott and Shackleton's antagonisms are well documented. Reading through the letters and diaries, it is clear that although Shackleton and Scott respected one another they were never close friends. On that return journey it had been Wilson who felt the need to clear the air and he "had it out with Scott."[48] The exact subjects of the discussion are not recorded and it is only natural that, at the end of such a tiring and trying period on the ice, that tension would show through. Poor Wilson was stuck in the middle of his two differing friends.

Eventually the party moved out of the thematic landscape of Tennyson's poem for "Ulysses" contains no mention of safe return.

On 3 February 1903 the three men arrived back at *Discovery*. A welcome cheer rang out from the mast and skiers hurried out over the ice to help with the sledge for the last few miles. Rather than join in with the huge celebration dinner, Shackleton bathed and immediately turned in. Normally ebullient, he really must have been ill if he chose to miss the party.

The difficulties caused by strenuous sledging and living under pressure in close proximity in the tent disappeared. Wilson described this home coming as "every trouble lifted from our shoulders."[49] Animosity evaporated to be replaced by the intoxicating perfume of 'home'. As they washed their faces clean so the three were able to look at each anew. I have lived in a tent with two other companions who did not get along. After (just) 35 days on the ice, our return to civilisation, marked by a shower and a beer, restored the fractious relationship. Soon, Scott and Shackleton were reconciled, united by insatiable hunger. Scott was heard to say, just an hour after the end of dinner, "Shackles! I say, Shackles, how would you fancy some sardines on toast?"[50]

A week or so after arriving at *Discovery,* Scott ordered that Shackleton be sent home on medical grounds. It was a bitter pill for Shackleton to swallow for as Wilson noted, "...he was very keen indeed to stop and see the thing through [i.e. a second winter]."[51] He felt that he was as healthy as Wilson, who had been in bed with joint problems (sore knees, a symptom of scurvy) for three weeks since the return from the southern journey.

> How dull it is to pause, to make an end,
> To rust unburnish'd, not to shine in use!

Shackleton had shone; in particular through the dark winter and despite his illness he had acquitted himself well on the southern sledge journey. He surely hated that his route ahead was being decided by another. Here at the point of departure, where the physical separation between Scott and Shackleton began, the prospect of any future collaboration ended. From now on the situation would be that "He works his work, I mine." They were to become rivals, but never enemies.

In the future each wrote warmly of (and to) the other. Any rift did not fully open up for a few years yet, until the *Nimrod* expedition. In Scott's mind, there was only one factor in the decision to send Shackleton home; he knew that he was ill, too ill to remain in the south, far from medical care. Alluding to his chronic heart problems, Wilson wrote in his diary, "Shackleton has... more serious symptoms which need not be detailed here".[52] No leader would risk allowing an expedition member with such a prognosis to remain for another winter.

Rather than dissect the wider expedition for signs of the rift between Scott and Shackleton, we should look instead to the relationship between Wilson (a doctor of medicine) and Shackleton, and what this tells us about Shackleton's approach to his health. They had built up a great friendship and it is hence surprising that Shackleton did not trust Wilson's recommendation that he should return home. Throughout his life, Shackleton experienced niggling heart problems which he ignored, determined to overcome them with pluck and willpower. He refused to accept any suggestion, from a friend, doctor or signs from his own body, that he was weak, blocking the very idea of ill health out of his mind.

As he contemplated the end of his expedition Shackleton might have turned a statement from "Ulysses" into a question and asked himself, "Am I become a name?" Not quite yet, but once he returned home he knew he would have a tale to tell. He was one step closer to gaining the position in society that he so desired. He understood now more than ever that

> ...all experience is an arch where thro'
> Gleams that untravell'd world...

In his case, this was to be an untravelled white road leading south, which he was drawn again to follow some years later. For now, as he prepared to depart, he left behind a final contribution to the expedition. Into the carved wooden postbox that served as the "in-tray" for *The South Polar Times*, he posted a sheet of paper on which were typewritten the lines of his valedictory verse, "L'Envoi".

Postscript to Ulysses

Tennyson's final lines from "Ulysses" have achieved immortality in Antarctic history, not because of a reference in Shackleton's diary, but through their use as a memorial to Captain Scott.

> To strive, to seek, to find and not to yield.

Following Scott's death during his return journey from the South Pole in 1912, a memorial cross was erected by the surviving members of the party at Observation Hill, close to his Winter Quarters on Ross Island. It was a labour of love, as the sea ice conditions were so poor that Tom Crean fell through twice while carrying the cross to shore, and it took eleven hours to haul the heavy wood 1000 feet up to the summit.

At the suggestion of Apsley Cherry-Garrard, the lines from "Ulysses" were used on the cross. Some biblical verses had been suggested, but maybe no verse could be found that adequately and succinctly matched the rhetoric of Scott's diary. Scott had created a masterpiece of expedition prose. Once the tent containing the bodies of Wilson, Bowers and Scott had been discovered, Atkinson, who was leading the party, bent in and removed the diaries, watches and other keepsakes from all three. He then read, aloud, for the benefit of the rescue party the last few pages of Scott's diary. It had a powerful effect on all present as, standing in the snow within feet of Scott's body, Atkinson read aloud the words of the dead man. "That scene can never leave my memory," wrote Cherry.[53] Through his "Message to the Public" and final letter to "my Widow," Scott aimed to stir the nation to support the wives and families of the dead expeditioners, but

"To strive, to seek, to find and not to yield." – the memorial cross to
Scott and the polar party, Ross Island
(Michael Van Woert/NOAA/Wikimedia Commons)

simultaneously he created the heroic, sacrificial vision of his endeavour that prevailed throughout the rest of the century.

In one of his last writings Scott also alluded to "Ulysses". "How much better," he wrote "has it been than lounging in too great comfort at home," an echo of "It little profits that an idle king,/ By this still hearth…" Possibly this was the trigger in Cherry-Garrard's memory that lead to his suggestion of the lines for the cross.

Cherry was scarred by guilt after the death of the polar party, in particular Wilson, with whom he was close, and he remained tormented for the rest of his life. He had been sent with the dogs onto the ice shelf at the very end of the season in a last attempt to find and assist the missing men home. As instructed, he stopped at the One Ton Depot, just eleven miles from where they were eventually found. As he waited at the depot, staring south, he had wrestled with the thought of going on. Afterwards he was haunted by the "what if" demons. His suggestion for the words on the cross may thus be instructive advice for future rescue parties—do not yield. Cut into the hard Australian Jarrah wood, the words stand for posterity at a place to which Cherry would never return. Yet it was a situation that he revisited daily, the words on the cross standing as an admonishment and cruelly providing no relief of absolution.

6 "L'Envoi"

A few weeks after his return to *Discovery*, Shackleton walked across the sea-ice to board the relief ship *Morning* for the journey home. For much of the intervening time he had rested in bed. He would have found this a most painful period, ruminating on his failure on the southern march and his early exit from the expedition. It is at trying times like this that the muse often produces its best works. "L'Envoi" is the poem Shackleton left behind as a contribution to *The South Polar Times*.

In 2012 a copy of this poem, written in Shackleton's own hand, came up for sale at Christie's. This version contained several lines which were not published in the original. I have included them here in square brackets. This is the first time "L'Envoi" has been published in its entirety.

L'Envoi

Slowly, though touched with glamour, the winter night went by,
And we longed to see the sunlight sweep up in the Northern sky.
Still we wait in this icy fastness till the good sun sets us free,
When no longer the tumbling billow is chained to a frozen sea.
Then shall our hardened bows dip gladly once more to the foam
Of the Southward driving roller as the good ship strives for home.
Brothers, we then shall be parted in a world that is greater by far
Than this weird and wondrous region shut in with an icy bar.
We shall read then in other pages words fashioned with easier pen,
Each day with its list of changes in a world of busy men.
But our hearts will still be faithful to this Southern land of ours,
Though we wander in English meadows 'mid the scent of English flowers,
When the soft southerly breeze shakes the blossom away from the thorn,
And flings from the wild rose cup, the shining gift of the morn;

And when the scarlet poppies peep through the golden wheat,
As the stronger winds of Autumn march in with heavier feet:
And when the fields are snow clad, trees hard in a frosty rime,
Our thoughts will wander Southward, we shall think of the grey old
time;
Again in dreams go back to our fight with the icy foe;
The crash of the steel clad bows; the sob of the tilted floe
The tearing, rending asunder; the crack in the frozen field;
The grating beneath the keel of the piece that sunk sooner than
yield,
[Then the black lead of open water where the good ship gathered
way,]
[The seal asleep on the ice floe, the quaint small penguins play.]
Our run through the ice free ocean till the snowy peaks appeared,
Crowned by the gold of the morning, shod with the glaciers weird.
[We shall see again the Barrier's bold edge to the land of snow]
[Holding within its bosom the secret we longed to know,]
Then our joy at the furthest East where never yet man had been;
When through the curtain of falling snow the bare, black rocks
were seen;
We shall dream of the ever increasing gales, the birds in their
Northward flight;
The magic of twilight colours, the gloom of the long, long night.
We shall dream of those months of sledging through soft and
yielding snow:
The chafe of the strap on the shoulder; the whine of the dogs as they
go.
Our rest in the tent after marching; our sleep in the biting cold;
The Heavens now grey with the snow cloud, anon to be burnished
gold;
The threshing drift on the tent side exposed to the blizzard's might;
The wind blown furrows and snow drifts; the crystal's play in the
light;
And when, in the fading firelight, we turn these pages o'er,
We shall think of the times we wrote therein by that far off
Southern shore.
With regret we shall close the story, yet ever in thought go back,
And success for each comrade will pray for on Life's still unbeaten
track;
And the love of men for each other that was born in that naked
land,

> Constant through life's great changes will be held by our little band.
> Though the grip of the frost may be cruel, and relentless its icy hold,
> Yet it knit our hearts together in that darkness stern and cold.

His poem evokes and captures the emotions that many a departing explorer has felt, but has been unable to articulate. Shackleton rates articles and poems written at home and on lesser subjects to be "pages of words fashioned with easier pen". In "L'Envoi", conversely, he tackles a difficult subject. His diaries show that throughout his life he was often frustrated by his inability to commit to paper the passion and fervour of his thoughts. Yet this poem succeeds in doing just that; it is one of his best.

"L'Envoi" has two themes: love for brother explorers and the connected idea that the impression left on these explorers by Antarctica will never leave them, even long after they have left the continent. It is reflective in tone; most of the actions described are placed in the past. There are mentions of episodes of sledging and the winter night that has gone by. Clearly the author was looking forward to going home, but already missing those companions left behind. The poem takes the reader from winter night, through spring sledging to the return home at the end of the summer. It is an attempt to condense his feelings about Antarctica and the profound mark that shared adversity with his fellows has made on him.

Rudyard Kipling's poem of the same title (published in 1892) was certainly familiar to Shackleton. Kipling's "L'Envoi" to the volume of poems *Barrack-Room Ballads* contains themes such as the end of summer, turning to a new road and a long voyage home, which are all reflected in Shackleton's version. It is possible that Shackleton's verse, in turn, influenced another with the same title. Robert Service wrote a piece entitled "L'Envoi" in his 1909 publication *Ballads of a Cheechako*. This poem too is a recollection of journeys completed in companionship over trackless wilderness:

> We trod that leagueless land that once we knew.

Over time, Service was to become one of Shackleton's favourite and most oft-quoted poets.

Shackleton's "L'Envoi" captures his affinity with the team, revealing the element of his character that enabled him to lead so effectively in later years. The poetic voice is plural, written throughout as "we", not individually or selfishly narrated in the first person. His experiences of the long winter night of the south were shared experiences, and were all the more potent as a result. Shackleton felt emotionally bound, "Constant through life's great changes", to his brothers with whom he fought the icy foe. Not all men would have been able to reciprocate; some could not get along with Shackleton's way. But the sentiment was true of Tom Crean, Ernest Joyce and especially Frank Wild who would follow Shackleton to the utmost ends of the earth on expeditions to come. Wilson might have joined too, but for other work to which he was committed.

> Though the grip of the frost may be cruel, and relentless its icy hold,
> Yet it knit our hearts together in that darkness stern and cold.

*

"L'Envoi" has been the most difficult of all Shackleton's poems to investigate. Each time I thought I had discovered the original place of publication or the complete verse, I would find the poem missing from where it was supposed to be, or uncover a new version in a different location. Even pinpointing exactly when the poem was written has proved surprisingly problematic, yet it is important.

Despite the reflective nature of the lines, for "L'Envoi" to have been published in *The South Polar Times*, it must have been written before Shackleton left Antarctica. *Morning* was the only ship to visit *Discovery*, bringing with her the only delivery of mail for the season and transporting Shackleton homewards. The poem is therefore most likely to have been completed between

One of the several versions of Shackleton's "L'Envoi",
in his own hand (Maggs Bros)

his return from the southern journey on 3 February 1903 and his embarking on the relief ship on 28 February. Two of those four weeks were spent in bed, recovering from the rigours of the journey. Wilson and Scott, too, had to convalesce. Each doubtless reflected on their personal journey and contemplated the future.

I found in Shackleton's notebook from the southern journey a draft version of the poem. He was looking forward to heading home, as all the men were, at the end of the long march, writing lines such as "we then shall be parted". The original expedition plan was that *Discovery* should return to the north with all hands after that first season. Scott only began to plan for a second winter when he returned from the march and saw miles of sea ice still frozen fast around *Discovery*.

The recently auctioned version of "L'Envoi" contains a note above Shackleton's signature, which states that the verses were written on the southern sledge journey. It is likely that he composed the poem while on the march, and probably during the early stages when he still had enough energy for writing and before any feelings of humiliation crept in as he limply skied along behind the sledge. It is difficult to be sure exactly when he began work on the poem because (as he did on many of his sledging trips) Shackleton carried two notebooks—one was used as a diary and the other for various undated jottings. The draft of the poem is in the latter. Certainly during the most debilitating phase of his weakness on the return march Shackleton's diary entries are few and far between, and these would have taken priority over creative writing.

Absent from the lines of "L'Envoi" is any indication of bitterness, antagonism or anger at the news that he was to be sent home while others remained in the south. Scott delivered the bitter pill to Shackleton around the middle of the period between their return and the departure of *Morning*. If Shackleton completed "L'Envoi" after receiving Scott's orders, with which he disagreed, then the poem demonstrates remarkable self-restraint. How easy it might have been for him to have written some lines of vitriol, and he might have felt, temporarily at least, a little better as he posted them into the carved wooden box for contributions to *The South Polar Times* before turning and leaving.

The title of the poem confirms that it was Shackleton's postscript to his time on *Discovery*. An envoi is a detached verse, coming at the end of a literary composition. It can be used to convey the moral of a poem, a personal note from the poet or to address the work to someone in particular. *The South Polar Times*, over which Shackleton had presided as editor for five successful and popular issues, was essentially *his* composition. This poem was his valedictory address to its readers, his comrades of the winter past. Louis Bernacchi, who took over as editor following Shackleton's departure, apparently included the poem as an end piece to the very last edition produced on the *Discovery* expedition in August 1903, five months after Shackleton had submitted it. This was the proper place for "L'Envoi", at the end of the final winter, when the thoughts of all the *Discovery* party would be of home. Positioning the poem right at the very end of the series of publications also acknowledged the debt that the team of the whole three years owed to Shackleton. He would have been pleased. Bernacchi had written of Shackleton in his editorial: "His loss to our paper is a serious one and much to be regretted."[54]

*

ENVOI TO "L'ENVOI"

"It's not here," I exclaimed as I sat alone in the basement archives of London's Royal Geographical Society. The original *South Polar Times*, published in Antarctica in August 1903, does not contain "L'Envoi", not as the end piece or elsewhere. This discovery was hard to fathom; I had learnt, from more than one source, that this would be the place where I would find the first publication of the poem.

I checked through each of the volumes published on *Discovery* after Shackleton's departure: "L'Envoi" was not to be found.

On his return home in 1903 Shackleton attempted to find a publisher for *The South Polar Times*. With the blessing of Scott, who wrote that "it will be an excellent advertisement for the expedition and fetch a lot of money to pay for a third season,"[55] Shackleton aimed to bring the expedition's newspaper to a wider audience. As Wilson noted, "the paper brings out the more human side of the members of the expedition, and leaves the narrative and the scientific reports to do the rest."[56] Whereas today such a document would be snapped up, in the early 1900s it had limited appeal and did not raise anywhere near the funds Scott was hoping for.

A prospectus was produced, which included a sample page from *The South Polar Times*, a contents list and a reply slip, indicating that commitments to purchase should be received by 1 January 1905. The prospectus stated that the publication would be "reproducing the original, typewriting and illustrations, both coloured and black and white, in absolute facsimile". It lists "L'Envoi" as the last item in Volume 5, which was the last volume edited by Shackleton before commencing the southern journey in 1902. This seems an odd location as the poem would appear to have been published before it was written! I double-checked the original Volume 5 in the Royal Geographical Society archive: "L'Envoi" was not there either.

Eventually a publisher was found and the facsimile copy was produced in 1907. In Scott's preface he promises, "The owners of these volumes will possess an exact reproduction of the original *South Polar Times*..."

Even though it is missing from the original *South Polar Times* produced in Antarctica, "L'Envoi" does appear as an end piece in the 1907 publication. This, then, is the poem's first appearance in print. Questions remain unanswered, and a small part of me wonders whether this was a case of editorial subterfuge. Did Shackleton bring a copy of the poem home with him and while arranging publication of the facsimile slip it in, thus giving himself the final word?

Several more limited edition runs of *The South Polar Times* have been published since that first facsimile in 1907. The most recent was produced in 2012 by the Folio Society; this also claims to be faithful to the original and does not contain "L'Envoi". It is accompanied by a commentary written by polar historian Ann Savours. I asked Ann about "L'Envoi". "You raise a point that had escaped me," she confessed, and continued:

> L'Envoi does not appear in these [2012] true facsimiles and it must have been added, presumably in London, when the two *Discovery* volumes were being edited for publication by Smith, Elder in 1907. I had assumed that Bernacchi had come across it after Shackleton's departure. These volumes [1907] were certainly not true facsimiles (i.e. as produced in the Antarctic).

It would seem that we had all made the same assumption, namely that Shackleton had left the poem behind when he left Antarctica. Each of Shackleton's biographers has used the first publicly published facsimile editions of *The South Polar Times* from 1907 when referencing "L'Envoi". Ann concluded with the tantalizing challenge: "[I] must leave you to locate the original of L'Envoi".

It seems most likely that "L'Envoi" was added in London prior to the publication of the 1907 edition. Careful comparison of the typewriting in the original *South Polar Times* and in extant typed versions of "L'Envoi" show them to have been produced on different machines. Secondly, the poem is not listed in the contents of the original August 1903 volume. Additionally the mis-listing in the prospectus suggests there was some deliberation as to where the poem should be inserted. I do not believe that the later insertion of Shackleton's verse carries any significance nor is it indicative of subterfuge. It is still possible of course that the original was created in the Antarctic and has become detached from *The South Polar Times*, but like Ann, I must now leave someone else to try and find the treasure.

7 COMING HOME

Shackleton's great disappointment at his early departure from Scott's *Discovery* expedition in 1903 was partly relieved by the convivial atmosphere on board the relief ship *Morning*. He slotted right in, as Second Officer Gerald Doorly recorded: "What a delightful first class passenger he proved to be during the storm month long voyage back to New Zealand. He entered into the spirit and fun of our little mess..." [57]

There were only seven members of the officers mess on *Morning* but they were the most creative of writers and musicians during the "Heroic Age" of exploration. Doorly formed a productive song writing partnership with Chief Engineer J. D. Morrison. It was not long before Shackleton was joining the writing team, giving Engineer Morrison the nickname "MacKinery" (for "Machinery"). Doorly explains:

> Morrison and Davidson [*Morning's* doctor] were the only two Scots on the ship. For some time MacKinery had been trying to impress the mess with the importance of the respective callings of Engineers and Doctors, no other professions being needed according to H. G. Wells' book *Anticipations*. [58]

Wells' first non-fiction bestseller was *Anticipations of the Reaction of Mechanical and Scientific Progress upon Human Life and Thought* (1901). The volume looked into the future with surprisingly accurate predictions, including a dispersal of populations from cities to suburbs, a sexual revolution, the defeat of the German military machine and the formation of a European Union. Wells described how by the year 2000 society would have a "central body, the section containing the scientific engineering or scientific medical sort of people." [59] The doctor and mechanic on board thought this was a marvelous recognition of their importance. Shackleton and Doorly saw this as a great subject for a song and co-wrote the lyrics.

Scotland Forever

We are two mighty men,
MacKinery and MacMush
We hail from Scottish glen
Devoid of guile or gush
We have but a single thu't
Our claim that our vocations
Will rule the roost in time to come
To quote 'Anticipations'

Chorus
We're the Engineer and the Doctor man
We'll do and dare it's a mighty plan
We'll melt down scrap
We'll mix up pills
Construct machines
Invent new ills
With pride we ask who's greater than
The Engineer and the Doctor Man?

The calling will prevail
We'll whiten [hoops] for keeps
The merchant's we'll asail,
Shrewd lawyers, chimney sweeps,
Police and parsons publicans
Prime Ministers of nations
Will fade away beneath our sway
You read 'Anticipations!'

Chorus

The prospect should be bright
We're experts in our arts
We're surely men of might
But in our heart of hearts
A logical conclusion
after serious contemplations

Is simply that the big idea
Is just 'Anticipations'

Chorus

(The words lose some of their vibrancy on the page and are best heard on the CD "Songs of the Morning", a recording of Doorly's compositions produced in 2002.)

✻

To continue his journey home, Shackleton crossed the Pacific Ocean on board *Orotava* in May 1903, sailing on to Britain via San Francisco and New York. En route he was inspired to write the poem "Fanning Isle". This mid-Pacific island, also known as Tabuaeran had, less than a year before, become a cable station. Intercontinental wires carrying telegraph traffic ran across the sea floor and intersected here, a place where

...the Northern tale
Is placed in Southern hands.

Shackleton was a great fan of the "wire" as telegrams were also known. He loved the immediacy of the communication and would always hope for a quick reply. Telegrams were not cheap; later Wilson would write back when Shackleton was pestering him to join the *Nimrod* expedition: "don't waste more money in long telegrams."[60] There was an element of theatre in the arrival of the telegraph messenger boy, and Shackleton knew the impact that this would have on the recipient. This poem is homage to his favourite form of communication.

"Fanning Isle" was written at a bitter sweet moment for Shackleton. He was hugely disappointed at Scott's decision to send him home early from the *Discovery* expedition but at the same time was looking forward to seeing Emily. During the voyage home one might have expected him to write about his time in the south, or his feelings following his premature departure. But for

Shackleton, everything was to be found in the future and he saw no benefit in dwelling on the past. It is therefore surprising that he did not write about Emily, his return home or the prospect of marriage. Whilst creating "Fanning Isle", he took his mind off the events of the recent past and for a short time ignored the challenges ahead. The four-month passage home was a time for rest. If we are to take any message from "Fanning Isle" it is

> That every deed of Nature
> Helps to the finished plan...

The deed of nature, or God, or Captain Scott, that had resulted in Shackleton's early return helped with the twin roads of his life plan, namely marriage to Emily Dorman and further exploration. His illness on the return journey from the pole in 1903 would later lead to the greatest advance towards the South Pole in 1909.

Fanning Isle

Surf-bound, lonely islet,
Set in a summer sea,
Work of a tiny insect,
A lesson I learn from thee.
For to your foam-white shores
The deep sea cables come.
Through slippery ooze, by feathery palms,
Flies by the busy hum
Of the nations linked together,
The young, with the older lands,
A moment's space, and the Northern tale
Is placed in Southern hands.
So, green isle small and lonely,
I find as I think it o'er
That your place in the scheme of nations
Shows to me more and more
That every deed of Nature
Helps to the finished plan,
That starts with the lowly worm
And will end in the perfect man:
That the smallest leads to the greatest,

And your worth may now be seen
As the pulsing heart of the ocean
Goes by your island green.

8 MARRIED LIFE

On his return to Britain, Ernest found Emily waiting for him, sustained by his "quite wonderful and very beautiful"[61] letters. "I will go back," repeat some of the lines in Swinburne's "The Triumph of Time"; a phrase that could be applied alternately throughout his life as Shackleton returned first to Emily and later to Antarctica. The poem asserts that eventually "time" will be called for each of us. Emily had waited and time had missed out on a victory.

In the poem Swinburne wrote about a return to the "Mother and lover of men, the sea," for sailors, even with new wives, cannot be parted from the sea for long. Again, another victory for Emily as Shackleton remained on land with his wife for much of the next three years.

Their wedding in Westminster on 9 April 1904 was squeezed between work. At breakfast that morning Shackleton met Sir Clements Markham who, though retired from his position of president of the Royal Geographical Society, was still an influential patriarch in the sphere of polar exploration. Ernest had persuaded Emily to forego a honeymoon so that immediately after the wedding he could resume his new employment at the Royal Scottish Geographical Society (RSGS) and assume his new role as husband as they set up home in Edinburgh. "Never mind my beloved whether the days are dull or cold or dark, we will be all brightness and light in our little house and we will have such happy times."[62]

This theme of a house become a home, a cosy, bright place full of love and in which each might find happiness, is one to which Shackleton returns throughout his life. Browning's lines

Let a man contend to the uttermost
For his life's set prize

had become a motto for Shackleton and to him the prize was
such a home. He sought to be crowned with the laurels of fame
but that would not be enough without a steady home to return
to. Now that he had succeeded in the quest for Emily, he expected
her to conjure up this domestic idyll.

Emily refers to "those early, happy days" of their marriage.[63]
Life seemed simple at the time: her knight had returned from
his conquests in the South and they were married. Emily might
have been looking for the "happily ever after", a cliché she would
later describe as "morally reprehensible."[64] Ernest too described
this time in their lives as "so bright and gay."[65] His primary role
as secretary of the RSGS was to increase its membership (and
therefore revenue). He set about his work energetically by using
and making contacts. He knew that to get on in life influential
contacts were the key. He had gained his place on the *Discovery*
expedition through contacts and another had helped him to
secure the RSGS role. He may have learnt from Tennyson's
"Ulysses" that "I am a part of all I have met". In the same way that
each adventure added to his wealth of experience, so did every
encounter with new people.

Emily gave birth to their first son, Raymond, in February
1905. But it was not long before Shackleton's restlessness
surfaced and Emily's role as wife and mother began to change.
Their granddaughter, Alexandra Shackleton, provides insight
into Emily's view of the wifely role, commenting that "Emily
said that she never read her children stories that ended 'And they
got married and lived happily ever after'."[66] Emily did not want
her own children to think that marriage would somehow open
doors to a utopia. All relationships require effort, and Ernest
and Emily's required more work than many, with frequent
separations, financial uncertainty and regular house moves.

*

One of the poems that Shackleton read to their children Ray and Cecily (born in December 1906) while holidaying at Seaford in Sussex during the early years was an extract from "The Triumph of Time" by Swinburne. Algernon Charles Swinburne was a poet whom Shackleton had come to enjoy before meeting Emily. Swinburne's popular first series of *Poems and Ballads,* published in 1866, would have been on the shelf at Ernest's childhood home. Swinburne was a decadent poet and some of his themes of homosexuality and bestiality may not have been approved of by Emily, but would have been just the sort of illicit pleasures for a teenage Ernest to enjoy. Emily was later keen to correct a line in Mills' biography to clarify that Shackleton was only interested in Swinburne in his "early years".

Curiously, the main character of "The Triumph of Time" is a tortured soul seeking an anonymous end. This theme seems diametrically opposed to the positive sentiments generally favoured by Shackleton. Perhaps Emily's influence on his poetic choices also moulded his life choices, or did Emily turn Shackleton from a Swinburne follower, seeking lonely solace in the oblivious sea, into a forward-facing Browning aficionado? Browning's primary theme is optimism— not a passive, "trust to

The decadent Algernon Charles Swinburne, aged fifty-two (Wikimedia Commons)

luck" existence, but an active optimism in which one has to work for success, but it will come.

In contrast to the linear, narrative style of Tennyson and Browning, the eccentric Swinburne wrote in a spiralling style, beginning with a central idea from which metaphors were flung out, often intersecting again with the hub. Swinburne, who reached the peak of his career twenty years after Browning, built on many of the themes of Browning's works such as physical love and death, reworking them in his own circular style, but he never quite managed to take Browning's place as the poet of the moment.

For Shackleton, Swinburne's works had had their moment by the time he met Emily, but his favourite Swinburne lines hint at questions about Ernest's view of his marriage, family life and the pull which was to take him away from them. Here is one from the 49 verses of "The Triumph of Time":

> I will go back to the great sweet mother,
> Mother and lover of men, the sea,
> I will go down to her, I and none other,
> Close with her, kiss her and mix her with me;
> Cling to her, strive with her, hold her fast:
> O fair white mother, in days long past
> Born without sister, born without brother,
> Set my soul free as Thy soul is free.

On first reading it is easy to see how this poem would appeal to children, who generally worship their mother: to cling to her is the ultimate in warm, carefree security. One can image them acting out the lines; clinging, kissing, while Ernest recites. Perhaps he read it to the children in an attempt to explain his longing for the sea and his long absences.

The mixture of Mother and lover in the poem is revealing. Ernest did seem to recognize Emily as a mother figure, often signing off his letters "your boy", and she acknowledged him, even after his death, as "the darling boy". Yet on the other hand, he would call her "child", perhaps attempting to be the dominant, responsible partner in the relationship and also accepting that there is something innately childlike when two people are in love. There is a poetic resonance here as "childe" crops up in the works of both Browning and Tennyson. In these poems the term denotes a young noble man yet to win his spurs, but it can also be applied to a woman of gentle birth.

In Shackleton's copy of "The Triumph of Time" he underlined the last line of the extract: "Set my soul free as Thy soul is free." Was this is a plea? Did his soul feel trapped? Perhaps Shackleton's yearning for adventure stemmed, in part, from a desire to be free from the duty of domestic responsibilities such as the family's need for love, to be fed, housed and clothed, all the banal ties of life from which he could just sail away. Or maybe conversely, he wished to be free of the pull of sea, the "calling from the wilderness", in order to enjoy more time with his wife.

The poem describes the freedom of the soul of the sea that was both mother and lover. Did Shackleton perceive that through motherhood or perhaps learning that Emily's soul was more at liberty than his? Or was it perhaps even a plea to be joined, soul to soul with Emily and to travel away together?

*

After twelve months working for the RSGS, during which time he had attracted five hundred new members, Shackleton embarked on a new enterprise, that of standing as a candidate in a parliamentary election.

He stood in Dundee for the Liberal Unionist Party in the election of January 1906. Hugh Mill, who knew Shackleton well, reckoned that the explorer "viewed it as a fine adventure and a tremendous lark."[67] Politics gave Shackleton a new level of contacts and networking and as much as it might have been a lark, it would be a learning experience too. Shackleton enjoyed and excelled at the hustings and public meetings, and performed better than other candidates because, at heart, he was not a political animal. Where the questions were easy to answer, he trotted out party policy. In reply to difficult questions, he used a smokescreen of humour to side-step the issue. His answers won him sympathy but were not necessarily policy; they were more of a performance than an appeal for votes. Shackleton was returned fourth of the five men standing and commented, "I got all the applause and the other fellows got all the votes."[68]

He had entered the race with a safety net. Sir William Beardmore, a member of the council of the RSGS, had previously offered him a job. Beardmore, a shipbuilder and astute businessman, offered Shackleton the position of secretary to a committee investigating new gas-powered engines. He was a man whom Shackleton could look up to, and Shackleton also enjoyed the company of Beardmore's wife, Elspeth. The male voters of Dundee may not have been seduced by Shackleton's oratory but he could certainly charm the ladies.

Yet just as at the RSGS, this appointment was to last for no longer than one year before he felt the need to move on. For Ernest Shackleton, it seemed as though there was to be no settling down. In many ways he always remained the ambitious but dreamy boy identified by Armitage.[69] He retained that child-like trait of not deliberately setting out to annoy or hurt another, but sometimes lacked a full comprehension of the impacts of his actions on other people, particularly his family.

Ernest's attitude to the minutiae of life could be infuriating. Emily wrote that "he sat so lightly to the things of this world, and was big". He was only concerned with the big ideas, the grandiose plans. As such he would have left behind him a trail of small issues for Emily to pick up: birthdays forgotten, appointments missed and, of course, bills unpaid. "I looked after small things, and they rather stifle the soul," wrote Emily.[70] Over time, she evolved from a ready foil for discussions of poetry or business into a hard-pressed support mechanism for a man who thought more about causes and campaigns than methods and deadlines.

Ernest wanted to be the man about, and of, the house and yet was often not physically or mentally present. He left Emily to manage the house and family largely on her own, which was a strain.

"Lady Shackleton finds her husband's honors not altogether an unmixed blessing," reported the *New York Tribune*.[71] The strains of organizing polar expeditions are not only felt by explorers, but their spouses also. One additional strain in the fabric of their marriage was the perception that he should "settle down". Emily took it as a personal slight when "So many people say to me, 'but he could *never* have settled down,' and right or wrong, this hurts me." The widely held notion was that Shackleton had a "restlessness in him that made him dislike any 'Ties'."[72] Naturally, Emily counted herself as a tie and she interpreted any thought that Shackleton did not like to be bound as a suggestion that he did not like to be with her. She felt that her wifely abilities were being called into question and that it was thought that he was always running away from her.

The truth was that Ernest was *continually* seeking to settle down: to make just enough money so that "things will be alright". He worked hard in a variety of roles but gradually became convinced that exploration was the only occupation he was any good at, and that it was the only way he could make a living. Years later, Emily met and talked to Bryan Fell, Clerk to the House of Commons, who knew Shackleton at the time of his election attempt. Fell confirmed to Emily what she believed in her heart: that Shackleton would have settled had he been elected. In Parliament he would have found all the cut and thrust required to maintain excitement, a platform for his oratory and a ready audience, not to mention the position and income that he desired.[73] This gave Emily comfort and in her mind it disproved the "dislike of ties" notion.

From Browning's "Paracelsus" comes the riddle: "I thought that none, Could willing leave what he so seemed to love…" For Shackleton, "to love" also meant an obligation to provide for, and in order to provide he had to leave. It is ironic that the desire for a settled life is what led to his peripatetic existence.

"I often long to recapture those early days," Emily wrote. "I never got him again for myself". Their marriage had grown into disparate strands: her role at home and his away on expedition or on business—and sometimes away with other women too.

It is clear through their letters that whenever Ernest left, for the South or for destinations undisclosed to Emily, love remained. When they were able to have time together it was wonderful; "*how* I loved being there alone with him—it was bliss," wrote Emily, recalling a holiday in 1917. In his letters, he would refer to her as "Sweet eyes" and sign off as "Micky". "On the strength of those tender letters, our love was so complete in every way."[74]

During 1906 Shackleton set his sights once more on the Antarctic. During his twelve months working for Beardmore he had persuaded the wealthy businessman to back a new expedition to the South Pole. This time, no-one would send him home early; Shackleton would lead this adventure himself.

9 NIMROD

"If he has the face of a fighter, he has the look of a poet: one must be both fighter and poet to accomplish what he has done."[75]
   Daily Telegraph, June 1909

Shackleton conceived and led the *Nimrod* expedition of 1907-09, which achieved the largest leap towards the South Pole since that point first became a goal for explorers. Much of the struggle required to make this leap had taken place even before *Nimrod* arrived in Antarctica. This was only the second expedition to Antarctica be organized without the patronage of the Royal Navy or scientific establishment.[*] It was the first expedition to seek funding on the basis of a promised return from commercial activities post expedition, including book sales, lectures and the use of the newly-emerging cinematograph. Although patriotic in goals and public relations, this expedition was a private enterprise and that presented unique hurdles to overcome. As usual, Shackleton turned to poetry for help.

He needed more than a little help with *Nimrod* for this was the first time in his life that he was in command. He used poetry as a tool, a mechanism to achieve a desired result. Rhymes and verses were not just for aesthetic pleasure or personal education, nor did he consider that the enjoyment of poetry should always be a solitary activity. His love of poetry and of the spoken word provided him with support and a means of self-projection.

Meeting Shackleton in person for the first time was an engaging experience: "[he] held us as spellbound as ever the Ancient Mariner held the Wedding Guest," wrote Mrs. Hope

---

[*] The first was Carsten Borchgrevink's Southern Cross expedition, wintering in Antarctica in 1899-1900.

Guthrie, one of the Shackletons' acquaintances from Edinburgh society. Samuel Taylor Coleridge's popular poem "The Rime of the Ancient Mariner" begins with the Mariner outside a wedding banquet ensnaring approaching wedding guests with his wondrous stories. On this occasion it was Shackleton enchanting guests at a house party. "Do you love poetry?" he asked and Hope Guthrie continues, "...I heard the rhythmic chant of great lines".

Mrs. Hope Guthrie understood both the gains and the difficulties that such exuberant encounters could bring to the aspiring explorer who "must needs be in human contact upon every side and all the time". Such contacts might be with potential expedition sponsors or young men who were on the ice for the first time: "...and it may work him not a little woe if in his fury of absorptions [a Shackleton pitfall] he happens to hurt human feelings or failings."[76]

Shackleton was about to find out all about such hurt when, shortly after receiving Beardmore's financial backing for the expedition, his restless energy propelled him onto the train down to London. He arrived at the Royal Geographical Society to seek its endorsement of the expedition, but the wheels of this institution turned too slowly for Shackleton. He felt he was given the cold shoulder and bustled to Fleet Street that very afternoon to put notices in the newspapers in the hope of gaining further financial support.

It was here that Shackleton, albeit without malice, "hurt human feelings" as Mrs. Hope Guthrie had put it. One word appears more often than any other in the subsequent article in *The Times*: *Discovery*. Inadvertently, and as a result of his haste, Shackleton gave the impression that his plans were entirely based on bettering the records set by (and avoiding the problems of) Captain Scott's *Discovery* expedition. "It is held," states the article "that the southern sledge party of the Discovery would have reached a much higher latitude if they had been more adequately equipped for sledge work."[77] This was much more of a direct criticism of Scott than Shackleton intended, but it was too late, for the words were now in print.

Captain Scott had returned to his Navy career following the *Discovery* expedition—a career which, on the day before Shackleton's article appeared in *The Times,* had suffered a setback. Scott's ship, the HMS *Albemarle,* had collided with HMS *Commonwealth* off Gibralter and he was therefore not in the best of humour when he read that Shackleton was out to better him. Moreover, Scott felt that he had ownership of McMurdo Sound, the winter harbour for *Discovery,* which was Shackleton's proposed starting point.

Such a feeling of proprietorial priority is a complex concept, rooted in the institutional nature of expedition organization at the time, and in the idea of "fair play". From Shackleton's perspective, Scott had not expressed any intention to return to Antarctica and the only viable starting point for a sledging journey to the Pole was McMurdo Sound.

Scott and Shackleton began a long exchange of letters on the subject with the result that Shackleton promised to begin his expedition further west, in the relatively unknown King Edward VII Land.* He was thus giving up relative certainty for uncertainty. Scott, meanwhile, required that Shackleton should write down the exact nature of their agreement. Perhaps if this negotiation had been completed face to face, following the Guthrie rule above, it would have not required a written undertaking. But with Scott at sea and Shackleton busy all over Britain, a meeting was not possible. This contract was a promise that Shackleton would eventually be forced to break.

Preparations for the *Nimrod* expedition proceeded with the usual panoply of logistical problems, but Shackleton had shrewdly shortened the ordeal by taking the ambitious step of giving himself just ten months to prepare. The interviewing and selection of expedition members, carried out in his own

---

* Later, in 1910, Amundsen landed close to King Edward VII Land, and took an untried route to the South Pole. His start point was sixty miles closer to the pole than Scott's at McMurdo Sound.

capricious style, was one of his chief pleasures during this time. He noted that it was tricky to get the right men, those who could live together during four months of darkness, but his technique showed that he relished this challenge. Raymond Priestley was asked if he could sing. He said he could not and was taken anyway. Jameson Boyd Adams was invited to join one year after meeting Shackleton for the first and only time at an afternoon tea party.

Hectic final preparations were hastened further by a royal summons to Cowes Week, albeit a summons that Shackleton had engineered. King Edward VII came aboard *Nimrod* with a large retinue during a fleet review in the Solent. As if this was not honour enough, Shackleton was delighted when the Queen presented him with a Union Flag and the King invested him into the Royal Victorian Order. With a stop in Torquay, the ship then sailed south. Shackleton, who was to follow a few weeks later, gave the crew a final rallying cry: "Play the game." he told them. The simple three word message summed up every theme of loyalty, determination and energy contained within Henry Newbolt's "Vitaï Lampada", which would have been so familiar to all of the men on board. Meanwhile, Shackleton anxiously set about securing further funds for the expedition in Britain and other nations of the Empire.*

Mounting an Antarctic expedition from Britain meant sailing through the tropics. These voyages were slow torture for Shackleton who did not like the heat. His poem "Two Ways" was written as the SS *India* took him south through the Suez Canal, and is dated 12 November 1907. Apart from a few lines of love to Emily, this is the only poem or poetic reference during the early stages of the expedition.

The title refers to what he sees as two alternative ways of voyaging: slow and calm through the tropics, as in his merchant navy days, or south to his current work "with its strain and stress" in the Antarctic. There is no surprise in the poem's conclusion.

---

* He succeeded in acquiring funds from the governments of New Zealand (£1,000) and Australia (£5,000).

Two Ways

You may love the calm and peaceful days,
And the glorious tropic nights
When the roof of the Earth with broad stars blaze
And the Moon's long path of light
Steals in a shining silver streak,
From the far horizon line
And on the brink of the ocean's rim
Still greater planets shine.
But all the delight of summer seas,
And the sun's westing gold
Are nought to me for I know a sea
With a glamour and glory untold.
The gloom and cold of the long stern night
The work with its strain and stress
Hold sterling worth and sheer delight,
And these soft bright times hold less.
For all is new on our ice bound shore
Where white peaks dare the stars
There strong endeavour and steady hand
Alone can unloose the bars.
Then by faith unswerving we may attain
To the oft wished for distant goal,
And at last to our country's gain
Hold with out flag the Southern Pole.

There seemed to be only ever two ways for Shackleton: easy or challenging, with the latter leading to "glamour and glory". He would always take the more difficult path, choosing the sea over school, chasing Emily's hard-to-win hand and leaving a comfortable job for an unknown expedition. The most recent difficult road to be taken was, of course, the conception and execution of this *Nimrod* expedition, his very own enterprise.

The faith mentioned in the poem's last lines was faith in companions on the march, for this Pole could not be won alone, and only secondly a faith in God. Although Shackleton had chosen the hard path of organizing the expedition without the blessing of established bodies such as the Royal Geographical

Society and the Royal Society, any new lands found would be claimed for King and Country.

*

The final departure of the ship from New Zealand and her passage to winter quarters were the most worrying of times. Shackleton described it as going "through a hell of anxiety and I cannot write it..."[78] Although he no doubt escaped occasionally from the loneliness of leadership into poetry, few poetic references creep into his letters home, his erratic diary or into the book of the expedition during this period. For once, the sea did not provide its usual inspiration.

There is one exception: while *Nimrod* was sailing south, some of the sailors onboard attributed the awful weather they were experiencing to the fact that the scientists had killed an albatross. Despite having irrational rituals and habits of his own—for example always attempting to set sail on the ninth day of the month (9 was his lucky number)—Shackleton had no truck with this idea: "...we did this for the purposes of scientific collections and not with the wantonness of the 'Ancient Mariner', the superstitious must seek for some other reason for the weather."

In fact, Coleridge's inspiration for the albatross is likely to have come from Captain Cook's accounts of his scientific journeys south in the eighteenth century. Like Shackleton, Cook had no qualms about killing and eating the birds which he described as "highly acceptable". The association of bad luck with albatrosses stems from Coleridge alone.[79]

*

As Shackleton looked out over the Great Barrier, a wide white vista that leads to the Pole, he wrote: "At one moment one thinks of Coleridge's 'Ancient Mariner'; "Alone, alone: all, all alone, alone on a wide wide sea."[80] With him were just a handful of men, months of walking away from their nearest neighbours.[*] He may have been thinking of himself as their leader, lonely within the crowd, a sense compounded by the party's isolation in Antarctica. "Leadership is a fine thing, but it has its penalties. And the greatest penalty is loneliness."[81]

In his book of the expedition, *Heart of the Antarctic,* Shackleton chose to borrow from Coleridge as he struggled to describe the polar landscape. "The whole place and conditions seems so strange and so unlike anything else in the world in our experience, that one cannot describe them in fitting words." The solution was therefore to use words that were already known to the reader, the words of Coleridge's "The Rime of the Ancient Mariner".[†] Shackleton knew that the most evocative method of rendering the sheer power of the Antarctic landscape, the life-long bonds forged between men and heightened experiences that he and the team underwent was through poetry familiar to his audience. The regular use of poetry in his writing and speeches added strength to the appeal of his words, enhanced rallying cries to the crew and enlivened the retelling of an adventure story.

In "The Rime of the Ancient Mariner", the Mariner is driven by a storm towards the South Pole and finds himself in a land without life. Written in 1799, Coleridge's descriptions of ice and loneliness had henceforth provided the accepted and conventional images of polar landscapes for all English-speaking people. The idea for the poem came during a midnight walk over the Quantock Hills in Devon with Wordsworth. But the specific inspiration for the polar scenes came from the journals of explorers such as Captain Cook, the first man to cross the

---

[*] The French explorer Jean-Baptiste Charcot wintered on the Antarctic Peninsula 1908-1909.

[†] Coleridge's original title used the spelling "Rime". Some years after the first publication of the poem he "glossed" the verses and changed much of the arcane language to more accessible English, at which point the title became "Rhyme". Rime is also a form of ice.

Gustave Doré's 1876 engraving "The Albatross"
(University of Adelaide/Wikimedia Commons)

Antarctic circle (17 January 1773), and Gerrit de Veer's account of Willem Barentsz' discovery of Spitsbergen (in 1596). It is incredible to think that Coleridge had never seen polar ice (indeed he had never left Britain) when he wrote his poem.

Cleverly, Coleridge takes actual illustrative points from his reading and inserts them into the confused recollections of the Mariner. For example, the whaler Fredrick Martens wrote, "the ice came floating down apace... and it was very cold" in 1694, and John Harris described the variegated colours of ice in his 1744 collection of voyages as "like Chrystal, others as blue as Saphires [sic], and others again green as Emeralds."[82] In Coleridge's poems these references become:

> And now there came both mist and snow,
> And it grew wondrous cold
> And ice, mast high, came floating by
> As green as emerald.

The result is an accurate rendering of polar icescapes in the pre-camera age. No wonder this work became the standard reference for polar imagery as Shackleton grew up, not just for the public at home but for potential explorers too.

Yet when these aspiring explorers realized their ambitions and actually sailed among ice mast high, suddenly they found that Coleridge was no longer enough, for the sheer scale of the real Antarctica in fact exceeded the poet's imaginings. Fabian Gottlieb von Bellingshausen (the first man to sight Antarctica on 28 January 1820) recorded a berg 408 feet high, approximately *three times* the height of his ship's mast. It is not so surprising therefore that once they had seen the grandeur of Antarctica for themselves, "The Rime of the Ancient Mariner" appears only fleetingly in Shackleton's writings (and not at all in Scott's).

Another explanation for Shackleton's initial allusion to and subsequent abandonment of Coleridge's imagery comes from a contemporary critic of Coleridge, none other than his friend Wordsworth, who noted of the Ancient Mariner "that he does not act, but is continually acted upon…" In contrast, Shackleton was an initiator, or to put it another way, "The explorer is a poet of action, and exploration is the poetry of deeds."[83] For Shackleton, the poem may have provided some glorious imagery but the story-telling Ancient Mariner did not offer any practical tools for expedition leadership. Shackleton turned again to Browning, for both descriptive imagery and inspiration for positive action.

Shackleton also used Browning's "Childe Roland to the Dark Tower Came" as a reference point that would be familiar to readers at home to articulate his first impressions of Antarctica. This poem includes descriptions of an exotic but empty land and also reflects on the emotional response of the observer. The opening line "My first thought was, he lied in every word" suggests that now that the explorers had arrived, all that they had previously been thought about Antarctica was proved to be, if not to be untrue, then certainly dwarfed by the reality encountered.

The knight Roland takes a few steps forward into the new land and then,

> pausing to throw backward a last view
> O'er the safe road, 't was gone

Approaching the Antarctic continent through a belt of pack ice, the road behind mystically disappears too. As a ship pushes through loose sea ice, a dark wake is left stretching behind the vessel, framed on each side by rafts of white ice. This signpost to the way home is temporary, for not more than a hundred feet behind the ship the ice recovers the water. Wind and currents move the floes back into place and the route of retreat is closed off. As the physical path home becomes obscured, so the strange reality of the new land ahead heightens the feeling of separation. Even though they have sailed many weeks from home and may be thinking that they had arrived, the explorers are stunned by the vastness stretching further southward still.

> And just as far as ever from the end,
> Nought in the distance but the evening, nought

Alfred Lansing wrote in *Endurance* (1959): "It was as if they had suddenly emerged into infinity." Such was the distance of Antarctica from their perceptions (in addition to the huge physical span) that there seemed to be no way back to the known world.

Shackleton's own description in *Heart of the Antarctic* continues in preternatural tones:

> There comes a puff of wind from the north, another from the south, and anon one from the east or west, seeming to obey no law, acting on erratic impulses. It is as though we were truly at the world's end, and were bursting in on the birthplace of the clouds and the nesting home of the four winds, and one has the feeling that we mortals are being watched with a jealous eye by the forces of nature.[84]

Had I not spent many months in Antarctica I would be sceptical about Shackleton's description of rapidly changing weather and the feeling of being overwhelmed by the power of nature, yet these are exactly the emotions which Antarctica elicits. He goes on to give an idea of scale missing from Coleridge, and to confound the reader further by writing not only that he and his men could see the sun at night, but also that there was more than one sun: "To add to these weird impressions that seem to grow on one in the apparently limitless waste, the sun to-night was surrounded by mock suns and in the zenith was a bow."[85]

Shackleton's passage is a conspicuous echo of the opening line of H. G. Wells' *War of the Worlds,* written in 1898. Wells' "intellects vast and cool and unsympathetic, regarded this earth with envious eyes" becomes Shackleton's line "watched with a jealous eye by the forces of nature". Later he refers to his party as "but tiny black specks crawling slowly and painfully across the white plain", an image reminiscent of Wells' observation that "as men busied themselves about their affairs they were scrutinized and studied, perhaps almost as narrowly as a man with a microscope might scrutinize the transient creatures…"

*

Shackleton had made one big mistake with his crew selection, and in a key role. He had saddled himself with an albatross in the form of Captain Rupert England. England had been recommended to Shackleton and in fact they had met once before, on the relief ship *Morning*, which had brought Shackleton home from Scott's expedition in 1903. England turned out to be too nervous for the pioneering nature of Antarctic navigation, his wary temperament contrasting with Shackleton's boldness. The strain of dealing with a nervous captain while at the same time attempting to keep his promise to Scott led to an unusual situation. At one point in the ice, both men had their hands on the engine control lever, Shackleton pushing for full ahead, England pulling back to full astern. In the end, they went below to discuss their differences while *Nimrod* and her anxious crew were left to drift.

The real problem was the promise Shackleton had made to Scott not to land to the west of the 170°W meridian. Sailing along the Great Barrier towards two possible landing spots identified during the *Discovery* voyage six years before, Shackleton was dismayed to find that neither place existed anymore. The Great Barrier is a dynamic floating ice sheet and, in the intervening years the ice had cracked and calved Shackleton's potential landing places into the sea. All that remained was an unbroken ice cliff, rising sheer to fifty feet above the water.

England was anxious not to be caught in the pack ice which was pressing the ship south against the Barrier, while Shackleton was desperate to land. Something had to yield. In the end it was his promise to Scott, made sincerely in the comfort of London, but impossible to keep in the cold reality of the ever-changing Antarctic. Or as Shackleton put it, "the forces of these uncontrollable ice packs are stronger than human resolution."[86]

*

It is easy to understand why Shackleton had mixed feelings as *Nimrod* eventually sailed into McMurdo Sound at the end of January 1908. To Emily he wrote: "I have been through a sort of Hell since 23rd and I cannot even now realize that I am on my way back to McMurdo Sound—that I have had to break my word to Scott and go back to the old base."[87] There are only slight hints in his writings about his emotional torment. In the difficult times to come on his *Endurance* and *Quest* expeditions, Shackleton would leave a regular trail of poetic clues for us to follow, but on *Nimrod* the pressure of decision-making during his first command was all consuming; there was little time to construct poetry, with one exception.

At some point during the "Hell since 23rd" period he sought a confidential outlet for his feelings and unburdened himself with a few pages of jottings into his notebook. To call these unfinished lines a poem might be stretching the definition a little, but it is clearly a seed of a poem. Today, poetry forms a broad church where structure, metre and rhyme are not essential component parts: ideas, inventions and innovation allow rules to be broken. This text, then, is a stream of consciousness, and of all Shackleton's writings this is the purest, unedited and uncensored. There is a crude roughness about the words and yet they are very special. Never before published and never intended for publication, here is a hitherto hidden insight into the mind of Ernest Shackleton:

All youths joys youths pleasures have fled without memory. The chord is broken and breaking roughly in the music comes the trouble and the wrong: and god knows what we would not do to have once more the careless freedom of the bright old days: when our sleep was a rest not a weaving of the things we would wish forgotten: When behind our eyes steeled to meet the world and its ways now there lurks the misery and the regret: and so thinking of what is missed by us in life we pray that those we love may never by action word or thought come to harm through us not only those

we love but the wider world indeed so that when we drop into the
unknown the harm we have done will not loom so largely in the
record of human life and we will try to make the few years we still
can count on better stronger and fairer to the rest of our fellow men
both from fear of any future but rather in justice to all to nullify the
dreary past. Youth that time in which the way is all before us when
each step is a revelation of some new light of nature when all we do
is but a prelude to better things and no way is too hard no work is
foolish and our eyes look forward gladly to each new scene finding
in the o'er turned page no sorrow only the promise of more pleasant
time when we breathe the morning air with laughter and delight
and no sin mars our waking thoughts no demon of remorse deadens
the first burst of joy that the advent of another day brings the sun
shines for us and for to make all happy we fling the days behind
in careless wise for have we not many years in which to live and
cannot we afford to squander recklessly these swift arriving days:
Ah such is Youth but the wine of the sun the pure joy of just living
is not enough to satisfy us when once the hastening years increase
their speed so that we in the middle time of life tremble at their
haste and clutch wildly at their flying feet: And what of those that
have gone: the record is graven in our hearts and you few indeed is
the record one to dwell [88]

The piece ends abruptly.

The juxtaposition of youthfulness and the feeling of careworn
sleeplessness strongly suggests that Shackleton was going through
a stressful coming of age as an adult. This might at first sight
seem odd: he was 34 years old and married with two children by
the time the piece was written. But it was the first time in his life
that he was responsible for a band of men, the first time that he
had sought investment from others in one of his ideas—and now
he had to pull it off while still learning his craft as an expedition
leader. It is both a lamentation for the loss of youthful innocence
and an expression of regret that this innocence has been lost so
quickly, with worries about who might have been hurt in the
process. This is an acknowledgement that in following his own
heart to the untrodden paths he has hurt those he left behind.
It was likely to have been a melancholy, homesick time when

he wrote this piece, for although positive images are found throughout they are all set in an imaginary past. Shackleton's optimistic mind (and pen) normally adept at looking forward had, for the time it took to compose these lines, deserted him.

10 TINY BLACK SPECKS

When they arrived in McMurdo Sound, Shackleton felt immediately at home in the familiar landscape. He wrote later that, "It seemed as though it were only yesterday that I had looked on the scene." The prefabricated cabin was unloaded and set up, tons of stores brought ashore and by 22 February 1908 Shackleton was "rid of England" as *Nimrod* sailed north. He had undergone an internal reconciliation over the broken promise to Scott, and in his last letter to Emily, he wrote that while his "heart is sore" his "conscience is clear."[89] His regret was that he made the promise in the first place and not that, due to *force majeure*, he had had to break his word.

Shackleton carried with him the volume *Moments with Browning* and an edition of Shakespeare's Comedies. From *The Merry Wives of Windsor* he might have drawn comfort from the sentiment, familiar also from Tennyson's "Ulysses", that "experience is a jewel, and it had need be so, for it is often purchased at an infinite rate". As each trouble was being paid for by Shackleton so he was gaining the jewels of experience, which would serve him well in the times to come.

The winter party was now complete and alone. Each man must have looked about him at the fourteen others, mindful of the small cabin at Cape Royds, on the edge of McMurdo Sound, in which they were to spend three months of total darkness, wondering what might become of them. None was unduly worried about his safety, but by midwinter Raymond Priestley had been disabused of his previously held notion that "a well managed expedition was nothing but a glorified picnic with a spice of danger".

Shackleton had done well to create a cohesive atmosphere.

The interior of *Nimrod* expedition's cabin at Cape Royds, as it is today (Delphine Aurès)

There was no segregation of officers and men as there had been on Scott's expedition, but it was inevitable that minor tensions would arise among a group held unnaturally close in trying conditions. An Australian clique formed; Roberts the cook attacked another member of the party for doing up his shoe laces with a foot on his bed, and Mawson had to separate them. Shackleton came in for a great deal of (initially veiled) criticism from Eric Marshall. Confiding in his diary, Marshall wrote that "following Shackleton to the pole... is like following an old woman. Always panicking."*

Such tensions were inevitable during the winter. The men lived in a cosy but small cabin, their only escape from one another brief walks in the midwinter darkness. Alongside preparations for the summer sledging season, there were entertainments to occupy the time. These included, as they had on Scott's expedition, the production of a book. Shackleton had edited *The South Polar Times* during the winter of 1902 and this time aimed to go one better. Rather than produce a single copy, Shackleton had taken a printing press to Antarctica. Frank Wild and Ernest

---

* This quarrel and Shackleton's leadership are fascinating topics, but outside the scope of this book. Leif Mills' paper "Polar Friction", and Morrell and Capparell's book *Shackleton's Way* provide more insight.

Joyce were even sent on a printing course prior to the expedition. The *Aurora Australis* was to be the first book printed in the Antarctic and around 75 copies of the book were produced. The material submitted was a familiar mixture of poems and stories, supplemented with illustrations by George Marston. Shackleton submitted two poems "Midwinter Night" and "Erebus", under his usual *nom de plume* Nemo.

"Erebus" was a celebration of the first ascent of the mountain of that name, a spur-of-the-moment mountaineering expedition. Five men took six days to reach the 13,500-foot conical summit that dominates the McMurdo Sound area, its volcanic, steaming peak can be seen from miles around. Erebus remains today an emblematic beacon for travellers arriving at McMurdo Sound from seaward or, more significantly, for returning polar parties. "The old landmarks are so pleasant,"[90] as Shackleton put it later when sighting Erebus on his return from the pole attempt. The ascent came shortly after the completion of winter quarters and at a time when much of the expedition was still in a state of flux. Plans and personalities had not yet settled. It was the first accomplishment for the *Nimrod* expedition and the summit achievement gave everyone, not just those who made it, cause for celebration.

Missing from "Erebus" is any hint of disappointment from Shackleton that he did not personally reach the summit. Marshall, the expedition doctor, wrote years later that Shackleton "never ventured up Mt. Erebus for he knew he could not have stood the altitude".[91] Shackleton alone selected the team for the climb and deliberately left himself out; perhaps doubts about his health, both in his own mind and in those of his doctors, lingered from the *Discovery* days. However, later that year he attained an altitude of around 9,500 feet on the plateau, with no recorded ill-effects.

Erebus

Keeper of the Southern Gateway, grim, rugged, gloomy and grand;
Warden of these wastes uncharted, as the years sweep on, you stand.

89

The volcanic summit of Mount Erebus
(Josh Landis/United States Antarctic Program)

At your head the swinging smoke-cloud; at your feet the grinding floes;
Racked and seared by the inner fires, gripped close by the outer snows.
Proud, unconquered, and unyielding, whilst the untold aeons passed,
Inviolate though the ages, your ramparts spurning the blast,
Till men impelled by a strong desire, broke through your icy bars;
Fierce was the fight to gain that height where your stern peak dares
the stars.
You called your vassals to aid you, and the leaping blizzard rose,
Driving in furious eddies, blinding, stifling, cruel snows.
The grasp of the numbing frost clutched hard at their hands and faces,
And the weird gloom made darker still dim seen perilous places.
They, weary, wayworn, and sleepless, through the long withering night,
Grimly clung to your iron sides till with laggard Dawn came the light:
Both heart and brain upheld them, till the long-drawn strain was o'er,
Victors then on your crown they stood, and gazed at the Western shore,
The distant glory of that land in broad splendour lay unrolled,
With icefield, cape and mountain height, flame rose in a sea of gold.
Oh! Herald of returning suns to the waiting lands below;
Beacon to their home seeking feet, far across the Southern snow;
In the Northland, in years to be, pale Winters first white sign
Will turn again their thoughts to thee, and the glamour that is thine.

*

While researching the poem I thought I had stumbled upon a previously unknown work by Shackleton, written at the same time as "Erebus" and entitled "Aurora Australis". This poem is contained in *The Antarctic Book*, which is a limited edition reprint of parts of the book *Aurora Australis* that Shackleton created in the Antarctic. As I read the lines of this "new" poem I realized they were familiar: "They, weary, wayworn and sleepless..." The publisher of *The Antarctic Book* had made a mistake. The lines are, of course, from "Erebus". When "Erebus" was printed in Shackleton's original *Aurora Australis* book it spanned two pages. The publisher of *The Antarctic Book* had mistaken the second page as a new poem (despite it making no mention of the southern lights). The new poem's title "Aurora Australis" was simply the original book's title which was printed at the top of every page.

The second of Shackleton's poems to be submitted to *Aurora Australis* was "Midwinter Night", one of only two surviving examples of Shackleton's light verse. This poem is ideal for live performance. No doubt the author would have wrung much comedy from the noises and multiple voices contained in the poem when it was performed at the celebrations for the turning point of the winter's darkness. The lines regarding the muttering of poetic rot are clearly self-deprecating.

By then, the early storms and tensions inside the expedition's hut at Cape Royds were settling. The men were learning to live with one another and their focus was sharpening on the goal of the pole. Even Marshall, who was not a fan of Shackleton, wrote in his diary, "Sh. composing poetry. Rather good on night watchman."[92]

Midwinter Night

The acetylene splutters and flickers,
The night comes into its own.
Outside Ambrose and Terror
Are snarling over a bone.

And this is the tale the watchman,

Awake in the dead of night,
Tells of the fourteen sleepers
Whose snoring gives him the blight.

The revels of Eros and Bacchus
Are mingled in some of their dreams,
For the songs they gustily gurgle
Are allied to bibulous themes.

And subjects re barmaids and bottles,
Whisky and barrels of beer,
Are mixed with amorous pleadings
That sound decidedly queer.

Darling you really love me?
Stutters one dreaming swain:
The watchman whispers "Never",
And the dreamer writhes in pain.

From the corner cabin a mutter,
The listener knows not what;
It sounds like "yon pale moon",
Or some other poetic rot.

Murder is done in another dream
And falls from shuddering heights;
Erebus rises to dance on the sea
And the dreamer flees south in tights.

Another sailed north on the broken ice
Just dressed in Natures clothes,
Whilst seals and penguins grin in delight
And the frost plays hell with his toes.

And some see tailors they knew of yore,
Stalk in with their mile-long bills;
And everyone when morning broke
Made a rush for calomel pills.

*

With the return of the sun around 19 August, temperatures and spirits began to rise. More activities outside the cabin could be undertaken, each leading towards the beginning of the great southward journey. "A glorious day for a start," wrote Shackleton in his diary for 29 October 1908, when, with Jameson Boyd Adams, Eric Marshall and Frank Wild, he set off towards the South Pole. The good weather did not last long. Soon progress slowed through a white-out* and stopped altogether during a day of blizzard. During this enforced lay-up Shackleton read *Much Ado About Nothing*. A few days later they encountered the first of many troubling crevasses: wide, deep chasms in the surface of the ice which are often disguised by a thin layer of snow. These hazards were to plague the party for much of their journey. The pony named Chinaman had fallen in while towing a sledge carrying the cooking gear and half of the fuel oil. They managed to extricate everything, but "only just in time, for three feet more and it would have been all up for the southern journey". "But when things seem the worst they turn to the best," Shackleton paraphrased Browning, "for that was the last crevasse we encountered." He should have added "that day" for there were to be plenty more ahead, including one so large it swallowed their last remaining pony without a trace.

Only rarely on the journey did Shackleton compare his progress to his previous journey along the same route with Scott, for they were doing well by comparison, "so different to this time six years ago, when I was toiling along five miles a day over the same ground". (By contrast, two years later Scott would measure his progress against Shackleton's record almost every day.) After only one month of progress, Shackleton's team passed the previous furthest south record. Perhaps it was the effects of the Curaçao with which they celebrated but at this point Shackleton's writing became rather florid:

---

* A white-out occurs when no discernible horizon is visible. The white of the snow blends seamlessly with the white clouds; the flat light produced makes orientation impossible and balance difficult.

It falls to the lot of few men to view land not previously seen by human eyes, and it was with feelings of keen curiosity, not unmingled with awe, that we watched the new mountains rise from the great unknown that lay ahead of us. – We were but tiny black specks crawling slowly and painfully across the white plain, and bending our puny strength to the task of wresting from nature secrets preserved inviolate through all the ages.[93]

His ability to visualize and then express the bird's-eye view of the situation in a pre-flight, pre-satellite photo age demonstrates a literary skill missing in other explorers. His remark that "the consciousness of our insignificance seemed to grow upon us" hid the fact that in terms of global exploration they were now the most significant pioneers of the century.[94] The moon-landing astronauts of 1969 had a map and photographs of the terrain ahead: Shackleton's sledge party did not.

As much as the travellers felt insignificant in terms of the "grimly majestic" mountains around them, so the mountains themselves became insignificant to the explorers as they focused on food and footfalls. Shackleton had to reconcile the food available with the number of miles to be covered. Equations balancing the twin devils ran constantly through his mind and diary entries, and the scales always seemed to be tipped against success. Several times during the march the team decided to reduce their daily ration, and then to reduce it further still in order to increase the number of days they could walk. This was a risky strategy.

Frugality was suspended for one day: Christmas Day. To their normal diet of pemmican hoosh (a stew of dried meat and cereal) and biscuit they added the luxury of "some of our emergency Oxo" followed by a tiny plum pudding. "Our thoughts turn to home and all the attendant joys of the time" Shackleton wrote. Alluding to missing his family at home he continued: "One longs to hear 'the hansomes slurring through the London mud'." This line comes from Kipling's "The Broken Men". Shackleton's men were not yet broken, although they may have been feeling a strain. They were now almost 10,000 feet above sea level having hauled themselves up the crevasse-riddled Great Glacier.*

In "The Broken Men", Kipling told how English outlaws, living in Callao (Peru) dreamt of home—"We sail o' nights to England"—but, of course, could not actually return for fear of arrest. In the often sterile atmosphere of the snows and in the stale air of the tent, our explorers shared the same longing:

> Ah, God! One sniff of England —
> To greet our flesh and blood —
> To hear the traffic slurring
> Once more through London mud!
> Our towns of wasted honour —
> Our streets of lost delight!
> How stands the old Lord Warden?
> Are Dover's cliffs still white?

Two weeks after Christmas, Shackleton realized the game was almost up. Unlike the outlaws, his party could turn for home; it was only their pride and determination which prevented their retreat. Exhausted and waiting for an improvement in the weather to allow a final dash south with the flag, Shackleton's ended his diary for 6 January with a Scott-like "I cannot write more."

By 9 January 1909 they had more than doubled any previous advance on the furthest south; they were just 97 miles from the South Pole. After planting a flag and burying a brass tube containing British postage stamps in the snow, they claimed the new land for the King and turned north. "What ever regrets may be, we have done our best," Shackleton wrote. Now the real struggle began, and they were by no means certain of success. They had started with 110 days' worth of food and had used 76

---

* Shackleton later named this after his primary supporter Beardmore. Whether it is named after William Beardmore, who backed him financially, or Elspeth Beardmore, who provided emotional support, is (perhaps deliberately) not clear.

days to reach this turning point. It was a calculated gamble, based on the sledges being lighter on the way home and returning downhill over a "known" route, but Antarctica is not known for her kindness to gamblers.

The return journey started well, subsequent diary entries for mid-January each recording a new daily distance record, culminating in an extraordinary 29 miles trekked in one day, on 19 January. Yet soon after this splendid advance the lack of food and the pressure of time began to tell. The ship had orders to sail on 1 March, and as this deadline approached so Shackleton's diary became more and more sporadic.

The principal handicap on the 750-mile journey back can be expressed simply: the four men were starving. That they reached each cache of food just as the supplies they carried ran out was a miracle, a miracle that was not be repeated two years later for Scott. A week after Shackleton's 35th birthday, the final depot was sighted. Adams and Marshall were too ill to continue so Wild accompanied Shackleton on a dash to the ship, which they reached on 1 March. Four days later, Adams and Marshall had been collected and the whole company reunited on board *Nimrod*, which then sailed north. Shackleton wrote, "it seemed as though a great load had been lifted from my shoulders". Soon, though, his shoulders would be weighed down again, this time with the laurels of the waiting world to which they returned in triumph.

*

Shackleton had striven "to the uttermost" for this prize, and found that his goal had exceeded his grasp by only the slenderest of margins. He had no cause for regret for "we have arrayed against us the strongest forces of nature."[95] Emily wrote that "one of his greatest qualities was that he never repined or railed at 'bad luck'". It was as though such a concept as "luck", bad or otherwise, did not exist for Shackleton. To justify his turnaround so close to the goal, he had one answer for the public and another one for Emily. Both are typical Shackleton *bon mots*. To the world at large he proclaimed that "Death lay ahead and food behind, so I had to return." This is a variation on his diary entry from 21 February, when already on the way back he wrote, "our food lies ahead and death stalks us from behind". Emily recalled that:

> the only comment he made to me about not reaching the Pole, was "a live donkey is better than a dead lion, isn't it," and I said "Yes darling, as far as I am concerned" and we left it at that—he never "made a moan" about anything.[96]

The press turned Shackleton into a popular hero, but it was respect from his peers that he valued more highly. First among them were Amundsen and Nansen in Norway, the Royal Geographical Society in London and Nordenskjöld from Sweden. The King conferred on him a knighthood with the words that it was "the greatest geographical achievement of his reign."[97] Captain Scott, meanwhile, managed to keep his opinions of Shackleton's broken promise private and attended his homecoming event at Charring Cross station. Sir Clements Markham (former president of the RGS) joined the Prince of Wales on 28 June 1909 at the Royal Albert Hall where Shackleton "gave us an excellent lecture", the first of many, many talks. His lecture tour started in October of that year and lasted for more than eighteen months.

*

While writing a few lines of poetry might have been relatively easy for Shackleton, he lacked the sustained concentration necessary to write a book about the expedition. Yet a book was required, and quickly in order to maximize financial returns while riding the wave of popularity.

Shackleton had been impressed by the reporting of Edward Saunders, a journalist from Lyttelton, New Zealand. His paper was one of the first to run, over four pages, the story of the *Nimrod* expedition on her return in March 1909. Saunders' first brush with polar exploration had come as a nineteen-year-old reporter when he visited Scott's *Discovery* at Lyttelton in 1901. There is no record of him meeting Shackleton on that occasion but when they did meet, after the *Nimrod* expedition, he and Shackleton obviously got along well and Shackleton offered him the position of personal secretary in order to take dictation of his book. In reality, Saunders was much more than just a secretary, he was Shackleton's ghost writer. "The pen was never a favourite implement with Shackleton,"[98] and so Saunders offered the perfect complement to the explorer's sculpting of the spoken word. Saunders accompanied Shackleton for four months as he travelled back to England, after which the journalist worked on the manuscript for a further six months of patient, painstaking work to which Shackleton was certainly not suited.

The resulting book, *Heart of the Antarctic*, was highly praised by reviewers who lauded the "skill and care with which this narrative has been compiled", praising "Mr Shackleton's literary energy and enterprise."[99] If the energy had for the most part come from Saunders, he shied away from any acclaim, writing: "Please believe that I have not the least wish to claim recognition in connection with the books."[100] The praise from the press was in part for the achievements that the book chronicled, but the key to it all was Saunders' great skill at bringing to life locations and situations of which the layman (and Saunders himself) had no first-hand knowledge.

All the heroic-age explorers used poetry as a resource. For Shackleton it was essential not only as a way of referring to landscapes and emotions, but also as a motivator as he struggled on the ice with "the vast strength of nature and the numerous weaknesses of his human nature."[101] Poetry was for him sustenance and fuel on the march, packed as carefully as paraffin and pemmican. One particular poem that encouraged Shackleton and several other explorers was Robert Service's "The Lone Trail".

11 "The Lone Trail"

Shackleton's voice comes into my headphones over the crackles of the rotating cylinder. At least I'm told it is Shackleton, but his tone and accent are unexpected. Two words spring to mind: "stiff" and "English". There are no traces of an Irish accent, which had been removed by his teachers at Dulwich College years before and he sounds uncomfortable with his audience. I wonder if this really is the famously energetic, animated orator. As Shackleton spoke into the microphone his audience was unseen and distant and he can have felt none of the reciprocal energy that he would have experienced on stage. The two extant recordings of Shackleton's voice[102] are treasures but I cannot help feeling that they seem rather artificial and passionless: how wonderful it would be to hear him giving a lecture after the *Nimrod* expedition, or better still talking to his men on the ice.

It is a measure of the fame which Shackleton had achieved that he was invited to make these recordings. Mass production of the wax cylinders onto which his voice was recorded had only been made possible in the previous ten years. From each recording, only 250 cylinders could be produced.

In both recordings Shackleton was at pains to thank his men. The tensions of the expedition were put behind him. He credited the men with responsibility for the success of the expedition and said, "they have been loyal to the very core throughout the trying times we've gone through". Clearly as far as Shackleton was concerned, frictions with Marshall and others were now in the past. He had hopes that the men would join him again as "once more they feel the wild calling them". My ears prick up at this poetic allusion, "The Call of the Wild" by Robert Service. But then comes the real surprise as Shackleton recites another Robert Service poem, in its entirety.

Robert Service, "The Bard of the Yukon" on the steps of his cabin
(Wikimedia Commons)

"The Lone Trail" tells of the beckoning lure of the wild places, written by one who understood them and read by one who had recently walked the loneliest trail on the planet. Robert W. Service (January 1874-September 1958) was known as the Bard of the Yukon. Born in Scotland, Service travelled extensively through western North America, settling to live in Whitehorse, Yukon, in 1904 when the town was barely a decade old. He was "sympathetic to 'rolling stones' because he was one of them in a very special way—a romantic adventurer."[103] One cannot help feeling that Service and Shackleton were kindred spirits and that Shackleton might have felt envious that Service was "liberated [by wealth] to take the open road of his own choice..."[104]

"The Lone Trail" mirrors Shackleton's own "Two Ways",

exploring a choice between hard and soft options. It also lends itself to performance. Service had begun to write seriously after being invited to contribute and perform a poem at a local talent night. Homemade entertainments of this sort were a feature of polar winters too. Service described his aim: "Verse, not poetry, is what I was after... something... the fellow in the pub would quote."

The Lone Trail as recited by Shackleton (who chose to omit the section in brackets)

> The trails of the world be countless, and most of the trails be tried;
> You tread on the heels of the many, till you come where the ways divide;
> And one lies safe in the sunlight, and the other is dreary and wan,
> Yet you look aslant at the Lone Trail, and the Lone Trail lures you on.
> And somehow you're sick of the highway, with its noise and its easy needs,
> And you seek the risk of the by-way, and you reck not where it leads.
> [And sometimes it leads to the desert, and the tongue swells out of the mouth,
> And you stagger blind to the mirage, to die in the mocking drouth.
> And sometimes it leads to the mountain, to the light of the lone camp-fire,
> And you gnaw your belt in the anguish of hunger-goaded desire.
> And sometimes it leads to the Southland, to the swamp where the orchid glows,
> And you rave to your grave with the fever, and they rob the corpse for its clothes.
> And sometimes it leads to the Northland, and the scurvy softens your bones,
> And your flesh dints in like putty, and you spit out your teeth like stones.
> And sometimes it leads to a coral reef in the wash of a weedy sea,
> And you sit and stare at the empty glare where the gulls wait greedily.]
> And sometimes it leads to an Arctic trail, and the snows where your torn feet freeze,
> And you whittle away the useless sleigh*, and crawl on your hands and knees.
> Often it leads to the dead-pit; always it leads to pain;
> By the bones of your brothers ye know it, but oh, to follow you're fain.

---

* Shackleton has substituted "sleigh" for Service's original "clay".

> By your bones they will follow behind you, till the ways of the world
> are made plain.

The legacy of "The Lone Trail" and the success of the *Nimrod* expedition are linked to two of Shackleton's contemporaries, each a superb polar explorer: the Australian Douglas Mawson and the Norwegian Roald Amundsen.

*

Roald Amundsen was among the first to congratulate Shackleton on the success of the *Nimrod* expedition, initially in writing and then in person when Shackleton lectured to the Norwegian Geographical Society in Kristiania, Norway, in October 1909.[*] Norwegians know themselves to be the premier exponents of polar travel and as Amundsen reminded him, "no assembly has been better qualified to judge your undertaking than the assembly you see before you."[105] The Norwegians were justified in their self-confidence. Nansen had led the first crossing of the Greenland Icecap in 1888, and Amundsen the first transit of the North-West Passage between 1903 and 1906.

Their judgement was favourable and unequivocal: "more than anyone else, [Shackleton] had managed to lift the veil that rested over Antarctica. But a little patch remained."[106] That little patch, of course, was the pole itself.

At a banquet given following the lecture, Shackleton rose to reply to the after dinner speeches; he was an excellent public speaker and there would no doubt have been a fantastic atmosphere that night. "I will never forget the look on Amundsen's face whilst Ernest was speaking," Emily Shackleton recalled. "His keen eyes were fixed on him and when Ernest quoted Service's lines,

> The trails of world be countless and the most of the trails be tried,
> You tread on the heels of the many, till you come where the ways divide,
> And one lies safe in the sunlight, and the other is dreary and wan,
> Yet you look aslant on the Lone Trail, yet the Lone Trail lures you on...

---

[*] Known as Oslo since 1925.

a mystic look softened them, the look of a man who saw a vision."[107]

Was that the moment when Amundsen realised that he was destined to go south and seek out the "little patch" that remained? Shackleton's use of verse transformed his speeches from mere descriptions of dates and distances into performances which delivered the emotions of expeditions to his audiences. Amundsen, notoriously devoid of human empathy, was being seduced and lured on by the spell of Shackleton and Service. A little over two years later, Amundsen became the first man to stand at the South Pole.

*

Amundsen and Shackleton never journeyed together, but of all the men who accompanied Shackleton on his expeditions one in particular stands out. The Australian Douglas Mawson went on to equal Shackleton's leadership skill, his daring pluck and fortitude *in extremis*. Mawson's first Antarctic expedition was onboard *Nimrod*, where he not only learnt the skills of leadership and polar travel from Shackleton, but also acquired a love of Service's poetry. All three would in due course help to save his life.

Mawson had meet Shackleton, briefly, in 1907 and applied to sail with *Nimrod* down to the Antarctic continent as a geologist and return before the first winter. Shackleton, in his usual style, offered Mawson a two-year post as physicist instead: Mawson accepted. The expedition gave Mawson experience of leading parties in the Antarctic; he was first despatched with Edgeworth David to the summit of Erebus and then to the South Magnetic Pole, taking over the lead role when David's health failed. Operating independently from Shackleton (who was laying siege to the South Pole), Mawson indefatigably plodded through 1200 miles of soft wet coastal snow to reach the Magnetic Pole.

His magnificent journey is often forgotten, overshadowed by Shackleton's own hair-breadth brush with success at the South Pole.

Shackleton introduced Mawson to Frank Wild, who later became his second-in-command and also to persons of wealth and influence in London, from whom Mawson secured the essential backing for his Australian Antarctic Expedition of 1911-14. Crucially, also, it was Shackleton who introduced Mawson to the role that poetry can play on expeditions.

Mawson respected and was exasperated by Shackleton in equal measure: "No-one could wish to be on the lone trail with a finer companion," he later wrote of him:

> His charming personality was heightened by this ability to illuminate his after-dinner remarks with passages of Browning and others of the great Poets. He certainly had a very fertile and poetic mind.
>
> But when it comes to the moral side of things S and I part brass rags as they say in the navy; and that is why I have not rushed into print to heap eulogies upon him.

The respect that Mawson retained for Shackleton and his widow led him "to say nothing on this more".[108] This issue which had caused such ill feeling was money. Mawson wrote to his compatriot Frank Hurley: "I would certainly never have advised you, man to man, to go with Shackleton."[109] This damning advice came not from Mawson's experience of Shackleton on the ice, but as usual from Shackleton's loose financial arrangements and his habit of making and then breaking pre-expedition promises. "To sum up his strong points," he observed, "I would say that S's greatest assets were a never failing fund of optimism, great determination, unknowing of fear, ambition and a fine physique. With the same strength morally he would have been the perfect man."[110]

Along with skills of polar exploration and leadership, Mawson honed his love of poetry while under Shackleton's command,

Douglas Mawson rests on the outward journey that would end with him crawling back to safety having lost both companions
(Xavier Mertz/State Library of New South Wales)

adopting the Shackletonian habit of dropping poetic references into his prose writing. The obscure phrase "parting brass rags", for example, occurs in a poem by Kipling. (Rags used to clean brass would commonly be shared between two Navy ratings: one would apply the polish, the other rub it off. To part brass rags was to dissolve the friendship or working partnership.) Kipling uses the phrase in "The Bonds of Discipline", an improbable tale of Royal Navy deception on the high seas, quite likely to have been on the bookshelves of *Nimrod* or at Cape Royds. Mawson later concluded his expedition diary with apt lines on the rewards of geographical explorations from Kipling's "The Merchantmen" (1898):

> We bring no store of ingots,
> Of spice or precious stones,
> But what we have we gathered
> With sweat and aching bones:

After the *Nimrod* expedition, Douglas Mawson returned to Antarctica with his own expedition of 1911-14. He was landed at Cape Denison, 800 miles to the west of Cape Adare, from the ship *Aurora* in January 1912. During the offloading, a box of essential stove parts was accidentally dropped over board into relatively shallow water. Mawson stripped off and after he had dived in to retrieve it found that it only contained jam. He said afterwards that he had "established a new record for himself dressing".

Mawson aimed to fill in the gaps on the map between the discoveries in the Ross Sea and Erich von Drygalski's expedition aboard the *Gauss*, exploring the area of Antarctica to the south of the Kerguelen Islands. While Scott was attempting to return from the pole though the autumn of 1912, Mawson too was engaged in a struggle for survival. To assist him home, he deployed skills and brought to mind poems learnt in the company of Shackleton years earlier.

Mawson entered what he called the Home of the Blizzard* as he ventured east from his winter quarters during the following spring. He departed on 10 November 1912 with two companions to survey to the east and was aiming to be back in time for collection by the ship on 15 January 1913. Good speed was made despite the large number of crevasses encountered. After several near misses with dogs falling in and being hauled out, disaster struck on 14 December. Edward Ninnis disappeared into a huge chasm, complete with his dog team and sledge. Looking down, Mawson could see a few dogs about 150 feet down, but no sign of Ninnis or his sledge, which contained much of the party's food. Mawson and his other companion Xavier Mertz thus faced the prospect of 320 miles of travel back to base with only ten days of food remaining. They had no food for the remaining dogs and as their route was inland there was no prospect of hunting for seals.

They fed weak dog to strong dog and also ate dog themselves including the animals' livers, not realizing that the organ contained harmfully high levels of Vitamin A. This caused dysentery, nausea, vomiting, delirium and eventually death. Believing it to be efficacious, Mawson fed some of his portion of the liver to his weaker companion Mertz. By doing so he was unwittingly killing his companion and saving himself.

Mertz eventually died on 8 January, leaving Mawson to struggle on alone. With skin peeling from his thighs and scrotum, he walked on for a month: bowlegged, with bandages holding the soles of his feet on, and pulling a sledge he had shortened using his penknife. Each day he grew weaker, hungrier and more desperate at the thought of missing the ship and spending a second winter, this time alone, at Cape Denison. Yet he did not to give in and succeeded in reaching the cape despite falling into crevasses on the way. On arrival, his disfigured face was so

---

* *The Home of the Blizzard* was to become the title of his book of the expedition. This phrase is apt, for his camp was located in the windiest spot in Antarctica, where topography funnels fierce drainage winds from the plateau down to the coast, with gusts regularly exceeding 100 knots.

unrecognizable that the men (who had volunteered to remain behind in case of any survivors) asked, "which one are you?"

Survival in such situations is a psychological game. Would it not be better, he thought, "to enjoy life for a few days, sleeping and eating my fill until the provisions gave out?" Mawson checked himself, and "thought of Service's lines".[111] His apprenticeship under Shackleton served him well. Throughout the harrowing, lonely march he had the poetry of Robert Service for company, in particular, "The Quitter":

> When you're lost in the Wild, and you're scared as a child,
> And Death looks you bang in the eye,
> And you're sore as a boil, it's according to Hoyle
> To cock your revolver and… die.
> But the Code of a Man says: "Fight all you can,"
> And self-dissolution is barred.
> In hunger and woe, oh, it's easy to blow…
> It's the hell-served-for-breakfast that's hard.
>
> "You're sick of the game!" Well, now, that's a shame.
> You're young and you're brave and you're bright.
> "You've had a raw deal!" I know—but don't squeal,
> Buck up, do your damnedest, and fight.
> It's the plugging away that will win you the day,
> So don't be a piker, old pard!
> Just draw on your grit; it's so easy to quit:
> It's the keeping-your-chin-up that's hard.
>
> It's easy to cry that you're beaten—and die;
> It's easy to crawfish and crawl;
> But to fight and to fight when hope's out of sight-
> Why, that's the best game of them all!
> And though you come out of each gruelling bout,
> All broken and beaten and scarred,
> Just have one more try—it's dead easy to die,
> It's the keeping-on-living that's hard.

The last two lines resonate through the writings of all explorers who have come close to submitting to death and yet have been shamed by their inner consciousness from taking what would have seemed the easy path. It would have been anything but "easy to crawl" through the wet snow and yet that is what Mawson had to do as his delaminating and bandaged feet were unable to hold him upright against the winds.

A few years later, Shackleton himself was in similarly dire straits while crossing the uncharted island of South Georgia. After 22 hours on the march with Worsley and Crean, they sat down to sleep. Fearing that "it would be disastrous if we all slumbered together, for sleep under such conditions merges into death," Shackleton somehow managed to keep awake while the others slept. He was not ready for the easy route; instead, "after five minutes [he] shook them into consciousness again, told them they had slept for half an hour".

Returning to the recording of Shackleton reading "The Lone Trail", made in June 1909, the recitation is not word perfect to Service's original. As was often the case, Shackleton misquoted the poet slightly, or as Emily puts it, "he always improved upon the original".[112] But this time the mistake was prophetic. Shackleton changed "And you whittle away the useless clay" into "And you whittle away the useless sleigh."[113] Emily was right: this was an improvement on the original and how fitting for the man he inspired, Mawson.

✳

Just as Shackleton was beginning his lecture tour at the end of 1909, Scott announced his intention to return to Antarctica and attempt to complete the journey to the South Pole. Effectively this meant that Shackleton would be unable to undertake further expeditions to Antarctica until the result of Scott's journey was known. It was bad enough that Shackleton had "stolen" Scott's base in 1907, but there would be a huge fuss if he "raced" Scott to the pole in 1910. Lecturing produced an income, but gradually the work paled. Emily described the years of 1912-13 as the least happy of times. It was also the year that the news emerged of Amundsen's success at the South Pole, and thereby opened questions about Scott's progress. Shackleton's career as an explorer was on hold. A few business ventures were tried, and failed, including a mining project in Hungary. Eventually, more than a year after Amundsen's triumph, *Terra Nova* sailed back to New Zealand and on 10 February 1913 news of Scott's death broke to the world. Much as he might like to, now was not the time for Shackleton to announce an expedition.

Shackleton's friend Hugh Mill describes that time as one of "unrest". Emily thought she was the cause of their lack of money: "I am to blame... we spent a lot". Of course it was easy to be extravagant when separated from each other for long periods, as the times together felt like a holiday. Shackleton's *Nimrod* expedition expenses were eventually paid off by the government, but he still had little personal income. These financial troubles were one reason to contrive another expedition.

Emily was instrumental in selecting a poetic heading to sum up each chapter of Mill's biography of Shackleton. The verse she chose for this stage in his life was from Robert Service's "Lure of the Little Voices":

> Yes, they're wanting me, they're haunting me, the awful lonely places;
> They're whining and they're whimpering as if each had a soul;
> They're calling from the wilderness, the vast and god-like spaces,
> The stark and sullen solitudes that sentinel the Pole.

The lines immediately before this extract might well be the voice of Antarctica speaking directly to Emily:

> do you know what they are saying?
> He was ours before you got him, and we want him once again.

In a magazine interview in 1914, Shackleton obliquely summed up the period between the end of the *Nimrod* expedition in mid-1909 and the departure of *Endurance* in mid-1914:

The explorer must have the vision of the future ever before him, a vision that is not dimmed by toil and struggle and disappointment. He must look beyond the praise of the world and the achievement of the moment and to the yet untrodden paths.[114]

With these heroic sentiments in mind, he now proposed a project so ambitious and improbable that it became magnetically attractive to everyone of like mind. "I feel that another expedition, unless it crosses the continent, is not much," he wrote to Emily.

Shackleton proposed to do just that.

12 *SOUTH*

"We are able to announce today, with a satisfaction which will be universally shared, that Sir Ernest Shackleton will lead a new expedition to the South Pole next year," exulted *The Times*.[115] Shackleton explained in his prospectus that his third expedition aimed to make "the first crossing of the Antarctic continent, from sea to sea via the Pole". This journey of 1500 miles, the first half of which was over unknown terrain, was a tall order, even for "the distinguished explorer," *The Times* conceded.

Shackleton's ship *Endurance*, named for his family motto *Fortitudine vincimus*, Through Endurance we Conquer, arrived at South Georgia in November 1914. At Grytviken there was time to pause and reflect after eleven frenetic months of preparations. At this point in an expedition, most explorers are excited and ready for the challenge but they are also mindful of the discomforts and dangers ahead and question their own motives. Shackleton was no exception.

We know of his drive to be recognized and to have what he termed "position". Since the saga of Scott and Amundsen's "race" the polar picture had changed. With the death of Wilson and Scott, Shackleton was now the only survivor of the 1902 *Discovery* expedition's southern party. His own furthest south record of 1909 had been broken and the new record could not be bettered. His business schemes, including mines in Hungary and a tobacco company, had come to nought. His notional value as a star explorer was diminishing, and the stress of debts was increasing. As Shackleton contemplated returning south he wrote, "I feel much older and a bit weary," but he hoped that "perhaps the Antarctic will make me young again."[116]

Certainly the idea of crossing the continent was one that he had first thought of in younger days. A small sledgeable boat, named *Raymond* after his son, had been procured for the purpose and then accidentally left behind during the *Nimrod* expedition. Shackleton had contemplated crossing the continent as early as 1906.

The draw of white, wild places is deep-seated; it is not only motivated by shallow cravings of flag planting and fame. It has been said that one can leave Antarctica, but it will never leave you. Shackleton had a poetic reference that articulated this feeling too. He wrote in his diary on 5 December 1914 as *Endurance* left South Georgia, the first verse of a poem by St. John Lucas, called "The Ship of Fools":

The Ship of Fools

We were the fools who could not rest
In the dull earth we left behind.
But burned with passion for the South.
And drank strange frenzy from the wind.
The world where wise men sit at ease,
Fades from my unregretful eyes
And blind across uncharted seas
We stagger on our enterprise.

The poem neatly sums up Shackleton's restlessness, and the magnetic pull of Antarctica. As usual, he was not shy to change the poets words to suit his own ends, in this case inserting "South" in place of the original "West". He had experienced the world of business where men sit at ease and had found it wanting. For Shackleton, uncharted territories were far more appealing. The poem clearly lodged itself in Shackleton's head for it appears twice more in his own handwriting at the end of the expedition. Two families in the Chilean town of Punta Arenas provided Shackleton with accommodation during the rescue attempts of his men from Elephant Island. He added the poem as he signed the visitors' books of Mr. and Mrs. Francisco Campos and Alan

113

McDonald in July 1916.

Lucas' poem was first published in *The Spectator* in December 1907, right about the time when Shackleton and the *Nimrod* were preparing to leave New Zealand for Antarctica. A few weeks later, the *Evening Post* republished the poem with a commentary. "...the reader will inevitably be reminded of another little company of explorers, who, in their tiny ship ...have just left our shores for the unknown South." The next line explains why this poem may have lodged in Shackleton's mind for all those years. The poem "suggests Tennyson's Ulysses and also The Ancient Mariner of Coleridge." and "compares not unfavourably with these classic poems"[117]

The Ship of Fools was a title first used in 1494 for a poem by Sebastian Brandt that presents an allegory in which fools steer a ship full of more fools towards a fools' paradise. Was the *Endurance* enterprise foolish? Certainly there were many at home who had suggested as much. Sir Clements Markham, cosy in London, believed that this expedition was all about Shackleton seeking publicity. For his part, Shackleton would have taken only selective notice of the wise men sitting at ease. He had benefited from maintaining Markham as an ally but, as leader of an independent expedition, he did not have to follow Markham's instructions as Scott did.

Shackleton did worry about the words of men in an altogether harder position. The weather-beaten whalers in South Georgia told him that this was the worst year for ice in the Weddell Sea that they could remember. This sea ice would first trap and then crush *Endurance*. Shackleton did not yet know it, but because of the ice he would be staggering back into Stromness on South Georgia 520 days later, having not set foot on Antarctica and having only been on dry land for six days.

The incredible story of the *Endurance* expedition is now famous both in print and on screen but to tell the story for the first time Shackleton turned once more to his trusted friend Edward Saunders with whom he had collaborated on the book of the *Nimrod* expedition, *Heart of the Antarctic*. This time, Saunders took on an even greater share of the work. Shackleton was worn down by the expedition, keen to get home and also eager to contribute to the war effort, but he had business to attend to first. As usual he had the expedition's debts to clear, engagements and lecturing commitments to keep and the long journey home to Britain. Saunders described their writing routine: "on boats and trains, at odd hours in the intervals of his many engagements, he told me the important parts of his new story". Consequently, a large portion of the new book *South* was written by Saunders, who nonetheless declined the invitation to be credited as editor of the book. Of course he would have been proud to be associated with the books, but "I should feel guilty of disloyalty to my friend if I made any claim."[118] Saunders died within a year of writing these words and his role in shaping Shackleton's prose for the page has remained largely hidden, as he had wished.

Saunders was given access to diaries, had brief interviews with Shackleton and then he was left to get on with the writing. Their previous close collaboration had created a rapport between the two men and Saunders knew intimately the man for whom he was ghosting. Yet he could not match Shackleton's poetic eloquence. The first three chapters of *South* are a gallop through the initial months of the voyage and the winter in the ice but they are also a slow crescendo of tension, leading to the sinking of *Endurance*.

A limited amount of equipment could be saved from the sinking ship. Everything that was to be taken had to be carried, and therefore weight had to be reduced. Rather than take a whole Bible, Shackleton selected two pages to tear out and keep (at the same time he also left gold sovereigns on the ice—too heavy to carry and of no use in his current predicament). The first leaf chosen was the dedication from the inside front page of the Bible presented "to the Crew of the *Endurance*" by Queen Alexandra, where she commends the men to the Lord's keeping. This was a logical choice, as the page would be a lucky talisman. Virtually

Even the dogs seem to realize the gravity of the situation as
Endurance sinks beneath the ice
(Library of Congress, Washington DC)

weightless, it was folded neatly into four and kept unnoticed in the explorer's breast pocket. Patriotic loyalty would have also been a factor in this choice: in Edwardian Britain one did not dispose lightly of a gift from the Queen.

Just as Shackleton had a habit of slightly misquoting poems to better fit a situation, Queen Alexandra slightly altered the two lines from the sailor's hymn *Eternal Father Strong to Save* which she penned into the flyleaf:

> Oh Listen when we cry to Thee,
> For those in peril on the sea.

When William Whiting wrote the original lines in 1860, he used the phrase "Oh hear us when we cry to thee." *The Magazine of the British and Foreign Sailors Society* of September 1914 was sent by the General Secretary Rev. E. W. Matthews to Lady Shackleton. It contains an article with a print of the frontispiece that includes the inscription from Queen Alexandra. The magazine proposed that her substitution of "listen" for the original "hear" is a deliberate change to give the text more warmth, and suggested it was evocative of a parent listening out for children.[119]

The other page of the Bible that Shackleton kept was the wonderful page of Job containing the verse:

> Out of whose womb came the ice?
> And the hoary frost of Heaven, who hath gendered it?
> The waters are hid as with a stone,
> And the face of the deep is frozen.[120]

The Bible contains very few references to ice (they are all in Job) and it is easy to see why this passage appealed to Shackleton. It is God's voice speaking out of a storm, upbraiding Job for attempting to second-guess the mind of God. God expected Job to "brace yourself like a man,"[121] and acknowledge the all powerful nature of He who created the hoary frost and froze the sea to ice. Shackleton drew comfort from the thought that even at the ends of the earth, his God was still there. He even felt that through his expeditions he had "seen God", and this phrase is one he saves for his summary of the whole *Endurance* experience.

Despite his father's encouragement and his religious zeal as a youth, the Bible was not normally Shackleton's first choice of reading. In *South*, he mentioned two complete volumes that he salvaged from the sinking *Endurance*, "a copy of Browning and one of 'The Ancient Mariner'". He continued: "On reading the latter we sympathised with him and wondered what he had done with the albatross; it would have made a very welcome addition to our larder." (Albatross did supplement their larder a little later.)

Perhaps this poem was chosen because the Mariner, despite being stalked by death still managed to make it home from Antarctic horrors. One particular passage was to prove prophetic when Shackleton staggered ashore on South Georgia after sixteen days cramped in the lifeboat *James Caird:*

And now, all in my own country,
I stood on the firm land!
The Hermit stepped forth from the boat,
And scarcely he could stand.

Both the book of Job and Coleridge's poem have punishment as a central theme. For Job, there was no reason for punishment; he had done nothing wrong (in fact, he had led a blameless life). The Ancient Mariner conversely deserved his humiliating punishment for shooting the albatross. Shackleton, on the ice watching *Endurance* sink, must have wondered how he and his men would escape punishment for their Antarctic folly.

Ah! well-a-day! what evil looks
Had I from old and young!
Instead of the cross, the Albatross
About my neck was hung.

Of course the greatest comfort to Shackleton at such a time would have been the works of Browning, which above all other poetry formed the background verses to his life. No doubt he would have taken this volume from the many books on the shelves in his cabin, which also served as the ship's library. Shackleton enjoyed this arrangement as it meant that sailors and officers alike would call in to collect or return books. It was an opportunity for informal chat, initially about the book maybe, but the discussion could open up. In this way, Shackleton was able to keep abreast of the moods and feelings of individual sailors and the ship's company as a whole.[122]

*

Zooming in on Frank Hurley's photograph of the interior of Shackleton's cabin, I wanted to discover the books that he had chosen for his library. I could just make out some words on the spines of the volumes. Many of the books are reference works, including several dictionaries and the *Encyclopaedia Britannica* taking up the whole of the bottom shelf. Next to a *Whitaker's Almanac* one can see the word "Works" but whose works remains unclear. On the second shelf, behind a tin of cigarettes (Shackleton was both a smoker of and shareholder in The Tabard Cigarette Company), lurks a Coleridge. Could this be the volume containing "The Rime of the Ancient Mariner" that he took with him?

Frank Hurley recalled how "we loved to hear snatches from Tennyson, Service, Keats and Browning, strangely assorted companions in that wilderness". While poems might have provided some succour they did not provide physical nourishment, and as Shackleton read aloud the lines from Browning's "Rabbi Ben Ezra":

> But all the worlds thumb,
> And finger failed to plumb...

one of the men remarked, "couldn't we do with some plumb duffs now?"[123]

119

As the narrative of *South* progressed beyond the first few chapters, Shackleton's distinctive style gradually emerged. Poetic quotations and allusions increase. Many are not in quotation marks and it is likely that during the dictation Shackleton assumed that Saunders would recognize that some of the words and phrases he used were quotations. Saunders, though a journalist, was not as widely read as Shackleton and thus lines and phrases from Tennyson, Browning and others slipped through unattributed.

The men struggle to launch the *James Caird* from Elephant Island
(Wikimedia Commons)

The first direct mention of a poet comes at a moment of frustrated triumph. After 800 miles at sea, the 26-foot-long *James Caird* reached South Georgia. Their thirst was quenched and a little rest taken before the six weary sailors attempted to haul the boat up onto the beach. They were in such a weak state that this was a near impossible task, yet the boat had to be taken out of the sea. For the whole of the previous night the men had taken turns to prevent the boat from being swept up onto the rocky beach. They all needed rest and they also needed the boat again to carry them a little closer to their salvation. Shackleton tells how "we waited for Byron's 'great ninth wave,' and when it lifted the *James Caird* in we held her, and by dint of great exertion... inch by inch we dragged her up."[124]

Waves come in groups known as sets and it is sailor lore that the seventh or ninth wave will be the largest of the set. This wave would lift the boat furthest up the beach, out of reach of the sucking backwash of lesser waves behind. In a moment of poetic muddling, Shackleton incorrectly attributed this line to Byron. It is in fact Longfellow's "ninth wave" from the poem "Milton" (named after the English poet John Milton). Shackleton would have enjoyed this poem for its nautical theme and also because it is a celebration of a poet and poetry.

Milton

I pace the sounding sea-beach and behold
How the voluminous billows roll and run,
Upheaving and subsiding, while the sun
Shines through their sheeted emerald far unrolled,
And the ninth wave, slow gathering fold by fold
All its loose-flowing garments into one,
Plunges upon the shore, and floods the dun
Pale reach of sands, and changes them to gold.
So in majestic cadence rise and fall
The mighty undulations of thy song,
O sightless bard, England's Mæonides!*
And ever and anon, high over all
Uplifted, a ninth wave superb and strong
Floods all the soul with its melodious seas.

A "great third wave" is mentioned in Swinburne's "The Triumph of Time", that same poem he read to his children on holiday in Seaford:

It is not much that a man can save
On the sands of life, in the straits of time,
Who swims in sight of the great third wave
That never a swimmer shall cross or climb.
Some waif washed up with the strays and spars
That ebb-tide shows to the shore and the stars;…

---

* Mæonides is another name for the great Greek poet Homer.

Regardless of the number of the wave, Shackleton and the five crew of the *James Caird* would doubtless have been feeling waif-like as they washed up onto the beach in Cave Cove. Perhaps pleasant memories of family holidays on a faraway beach turned this poem, which has suicide as its central theme, into motivation to redouble efforts and return home.

The chapters of *South* which tell of South Georgia and Shackleton's return to civilization were the first to be dictated. This dictation took place in New Zealand shortly after the safe return of the Ross Sea survivors. Shackleton was persuaded to get straight to the business of setting down his experiences "lest they might be lost forever," wrote his first biographer, Hugh Mill, "if the explorer found the battlefields of Europe more fatal than those of the Antarctic."[125]

Shackleton's mistake in the attribution of the Longfellow poem perhaps had less to do with the stress of the moment than with the stress of the recollection of the moment. Leonard Tripp, Shackleton's advisor and supporter in New Zealand, later described the often painful dictation scene to Mill:

> Shackleton walked up and down the room smoking a cigarette, and I was absolutely amazed at his language. He very seldom hesitated... I watched him, and his whole face seemed to swell, and I could see the man was suffering. After about half an hour he turned to me and with tears in his eyes he said, "Tripp, you don't know what I've been through, and I am going through it all again, and I can't do it."[126]

At times, the prose flowed from Shackleton like the extempore speeches he was so skilled at delivering, but sometimes emotions took over and he would have to leave the room for a few minutes. The break would give Saunders time to correct his shorthand. Soon Shackleton was back, knowing that the opportunity had to be seized, and the narrative would continue. It was clearly a process he would rather not have gone through, but it produced some of the best chapters of the book.

*

As Shackleton, Worsley and Crean neared the end of their pioneering crossing of South Georgia (having left McNish, Vincent and McCarthy at a place they christened Peggotty Camp on the south side), they spotted the distinctive folded rock formations above the whaling station at Stromness. At this point they realized that they were at the verge of salvation. Shackleton wrote, "but the worst was turning to the best for us". One of his favourite mottos had come true.

The lines are from "Prospice" by Robert Browning: "For sudden the worst turns the best to the brave..." While this poem would have been in the book saved from *Endurance*, the volume had been jettisoned on the journey across the ice. Nevertheless, the lines from Shackleton's favourite poem were impossible to eject from his memory. As he recalled the blackest moments of the expedition, it was the encouraging words of "Prospice" that came to mind.

This was how Shackleton managed to survive and bring all the men back out of Antarctica with him. His memory did not conjure up melancholy lines bemoaning his Job-like fate but instead Browning's active optimism. As he talked to Saunders, Shackleton went back to the time on South Georgia. The lines that came to mind as he painfully relived it all were positive, brave and forward looking. This was Shackleton, the ever ambitious and dreamy boy, now a strong man and escaping like the Ancient Mariner from his brush with death in Antarctica.

*

There is a very special moment on each expedition, whether it has gone to plan or turned into an epic escape. That moment is the time just prior to re-contacting the outside world. For many months, one has been bound together with just a few others by shared experience, dirt and privations; a team isolated from news, family and distractions. The expedition and these bonds are at this point a hermetically sealed package. It is complete and finished only in that last nanosecond just before the end.

As soon as civilization is reached, the seal is broken and with a rush of air the rest of the world swoops in, weaving in between the men, cleaning up, washing away and diluting the experiences. At this point, the expedition is both home victorious and lost forever; confined to memories that are inevitably going to fade. Shackleton later wrote that "Pain and ache, boat journeys, marches, hunger and fatigue seemed to belong to the limbo of forgotten things."[127]

Four months passed between Shackleton reaching safety at Stromness and reliving it all for Saunders to write down. Those four desperate months were full of rescue attempts to Elephant Island and a dash around the world to see home the Ross Sea party. Yet, as he paced up and down smoking, Shackleton was able to re-enter that painful time as though it were the present and (with some help) come up with a beautiful summary of all that happened. As he dictated, Shackleton took himself back to that special moment just prior to reaching Stromness with Worsley and Crean. The world had not yet rushed in, their journey of two years together was still intact and almost complete: "...we had flung down the adze from the top of the fall and also the log book and the cooker... that was all, except our wet clothes, that we had brought out of the Antarctic... yet in memories we were rich." The adze was used to cut steps in hard ice, the "cooker" was in fact a type of saucepan. Why they still carried it is a mystery, as their food had run out and the Primus stove had been left miles behind. The logbook from *Endurance* was wrapped in a cloth. This precious volume contained a berg-by-berg account of their two-year odyssey.

As Worsley "produced several safety pins from some corner of his garments and effected some temporary repairs that really emphasized his general disrepair," so Shackleton began to try to sum up his emotions on their adventure. With an echo of Job, and paraphrasing Service, he wrote:

> We had pierced the veneer of outside things. We had "suffered,
> starved, and triumphed, grovelled down yet grasped at glory,
> grown bigger in the bigness of the whole." We had seen God in his
> splendors, heard the text that Nature renders. We had reached the
> naked soul of man.[128]

Shackleton and Saunders' vivid descriptions of ice, sea, torment of thirst and treacherous pack-ice prepare the reader for this summary and yet one is still surprised by the depth of these enigmatic lines. Each line opens with "We", emphasizing the shared experience. They become progressively shorter, each more breathless than the last, the subjects progressively more awesome, just as the expedition had become smaller by increments: from a ship, full of possessions and hopes, to a camp on the vast ice, and finally to the boats with just a few items in the men's pockets. The numbers of companions diminished (though they were all still alive) from a full team at Elephant Island, to six sailing to South Georgia and a final three who crossed the island.

Shackleton was happy to borrow when his own words failed. The middle section in quotation marks is from Robert Service's "The Call of the Wild". Two craftsmen were at work here: the original poet whose evocation of cold wild places comes from his own experiences in the Yukon, and Shackleton, who selected and re-shaped the phrases. Service asked, "Have you suffered, starved and triumphed?" Assuming the answer to be "no", he urged the reader: "Then for God's sake go and do it." Shackleton had most certainly answered that call.

Here is verse four of "The Call of the Wild";

> Have you suffered, starved and triumphed, groveled down, yet
> grasped at glory?
> Grown bigger in the bigness of the whole?
> "Done things" just for the doing, letting babblers tell the story,
> Seeing through the nice veneer the naked soul?
> Have you seen God in all His splendors, heard the text that nature
> renders?

(You'll never hear it in the family pew.)
The simple things, the true things, the silent men who do things-
Then listen to the Wild-it's calling you.

Alluding to meeting or seeing God, and getting closer to the soul of man, Shackleton acknowledged how close they had come to disaster. Death had rarely been far away during the preceding months. All members of the expedition had aged and been weakened as a result and naturally the leader had suffered and aged the most. "Hearing the text that nature renders" was the positive counterpoint, working through such situations bringing the reward of enhanced self-knowledge. Each of them had grown bigger, through the strength that comes from being a unit that is greater than the sum of its parts.

"Man" also refers to Mankind, and the experience of the previous two years had brought out the "naked soul" and the very best in all of the men. Set against the bloody horrors of the Great War, about which they were still learning, the harrowing experience of *Endurance* would feel strangely frivolous. In Antarctica nature was the only foe and any man was an ally, while in "civilized" Europe the fight was man against man. This must have seemed inexplicable to Shackleton and his companions; they thought they had learnt all there was to know about human nature during their two years afloat.

In the baths of the whaling station "nature's text" became faint in their memories as the grime of nearly twelve months was scrubbed off. The close-up sight of God faded as beards were shaved and hair un-matted. While the marking on the soul proved permanent, it was quickly camouflaged. Worsley returned by ship to collect Vincent, McCarthy and McNeish who had remained at Peggotty Camp on the south side of the island. "We thought the Boss or one of the others would come round," they said as they greeted him.[129] The three men did not recognize their captain and companion of eighteen months although he had only been gone three days. These men were still wholly within the adventure whereas Worsley had now returned to the outside world. He had travelled only a few miles over the island but emotionally he was a thousand miles from the destitute three at Peggotty Camp.

*

John Keats, a much loved and quoted poet during the late nineteenth century, and no doubt one whom Shackleton would have read at school, makes a rare appearance towards the end of *South*. Keats was a Romanic, who often employed images and events from the classics. Tennyson was a fan of Keats and many of his poems use similar classical images. Keats and Shackleton both grew up in London, both went to a non-elite boarding school and both died young (Keats extremely so, aged only twenty-five).

From the poem "Endymion", published in 1818, Shackleton used a line to help justify a tantalizingly brief paragraph in *South*. Frustrated by the difficulty of delivering to the page the profound experiences of the expedition and borrowing from Keats, he lamented "the dearth of human words, the roughness of mortal speech". He struggled to explain the presence that he, Worsley and Crean felt as they crossed South Georgia. "I know that during that long and racking march of thirty-six hours over the unnamed mountains and glaciers of South Georgia it seemed to me often that we were four, not three."[130]

Shackleton was not alone in this feeling. Years later, Frank Worsley gave a lecture in which he referred to four men crossing the island. When the error was pointed out to him afterwards, he replied, "Whatever will they think of me? I can't get it out of my mind."[131]

This revelation, dictated during the same session as the rest of the chapter, almost did not make it into the published version of *South*. Shackleton never wrote much about his faith and he may have felt reluctant to admit that "Providence had guided us". He had kept the experience to himself, not even mentioning it to his close companions of the march until some time later. The paragraph does not appear as part of Saunders' draft typescript of the chapter, but on a separate sheet headed "NOTE". It is likely that the story was noted at the time of the dictation in 1917 but that Shackleton only decided to include it in the book later in the publication process, in 1919.[132]

Had this, the last paragraph of the last chapter of Shackleton's escape from the Antarctic been omitted, a crucial element of the story would have been forgotten. Many sermons would have been denied the reference to a mysterious presence guiding those who travel, and a poetic inspiration would have been lost.

T. S. Eliot, writing "The Waste Land" in 1922, the year that Shackleton died, wrote that he was "...stimulated by the account of one of the Antarctic expeditions (I forget which, but I think one of Shackleton's): it was related that the party of explorers, at the extremity of their strength, had the constant delusion that there was one more [in their] number than could actually be counted."[133]

Eliot wrote a small body of poetic work but strove for perfection in every piece. A Harvard alumnus, his pieces are complex, drawing on many references. *The Waste Land* is Eliot at his most allusive and obscure. This is an extract from *The Waste Land*, just a few of the 433 lines of this poem which had countless influences and uses several languages as it described myriad images of failure, written during a period of nervous illness for Eliot. True to the multi-voice (some might say disjointed) form of the poem, this verse stands alone, a non-sequitur with those that precede and follow it:

Who is the third who walks always beside you?
When I count, there are only you and I together
But when I look ahead up the white road
There is always another one walking beside you
Gliding wrapt in a brown mantle, hooded
I do not know whether a man or a woman
- But who is that on the other side of you?

Shackleton died nine months before the publication of *The Waste Land*. He would have been flattered and pleased that a poet had been inspired by and able to make imaginative use of his experiences.

*

Postscript to South

A major pleasure of researching and writing this biography has been making unexpected discoveries. Shortly after writing the draft of this chapter, I discovered that the Bible which Shackleton thought he had abandoned on the ice had in fact made it back to London. It is now at the Royal Geographical Society so I took the train to London to see it.

The volume is obviously well travelled. As I opened it a chasm appeared between the binding and the spine. Inside the cover is written:

> To Mrs Mclean
> From
> T. F. M'Leod
> Trans Ant Expedition
> 13.9.16

Thomas McLeod, an Able Seaman, retrieved the Bible from among the piles of belongings left behind and brought it out of the ice with him. Later, he gave it to the Mclean family, who generously put him up when he arrived, destitute, in Punta Arenas, following his rescue from Elephant Island. The Bible took one more journey. Miss I. Mclean gave it to Malcolm Burley, leader of the British forces Joint Services Expedition to Elephant Island in 1970-71, after he had given a lecture on his expedition to an audience in Buenos Aires. Commander Burley then entrusted the Bible to the Royal Geographical Society.

In *South* Shackleton recounted how he tore out a passage from

Job and Psalm 23. Also missing from the Bible is Psalm 22, which although not mentioned was nevertheless taken and carried with him. It begins with the familiar words "My God, my God, why hast though forsaken me?" which Jesus quoted on the cross, but it is in fact a psalm of hope, continuing: "he has not hidden his face from him but has listened to his cry for help." Shackleton managed to keep the pages relatively unharmed through the journey on the ice, the sixteen days in the *James Caird* and the crossing of South Georgia. Along with Queen Alexandra's inscription and the passage from Job, these pages remain in the care of the Shackleton family to this day.

*

A modern poem has been inspired by Shackleton's choice of the lines from Job. Katharine Coles spent a month in 2010 on the tiny American Palmer Station in Antarctica as a guest of the National Science Foundation's Antarctic Artists and Writers Program. The Earth is not Flat is her collection of poems written out of that adventure and also inspired by historical figures such as Shackleton.

JOB

He, not I. *Waters*   *hid.*
Beleaguered, *hoary*, everything

Leagued against. *Out of*
                 Heaven

Gendered. A woman
May be. *Whose womb.* Ship

Bellying. I believe
I'm safe. *Hid*   *a stone.* Ship

Dropping, rising
With a stone

Thirty feet at once. *Frost*
Of Heaven I know

No hardship. *Frozen*
                    Face

Of the deep   *out of whose* he
And I stranded.

Coles describes her poem "Job" as "Beginning with an erasure of verses quoted by Shackleton". She dissects the four lines of Job and then intersects with them, creating a meditation on her own rough voyage by ship over the Drake Passage to Palmer. The poem contains the themes of a face (and it is by seeing a face that we recognize, in this case, God) and of the helplessness of Job and Shackleton as they were moved by elements over which they had no control. Coles too must trust ("I believe I'm safe") but at the same time, "he [Shackleton] and I are stranded". In her case, she is stranded on board as a passenger, subject to the will of the sea.

13 THE GREAT WAR

Emerging from the crossing of South Georgia and back into civilization at Stromness whaling station in May 1916, Shackleton learnt that the First World War was far from over. He was preoccupied with his own battles for the time being, with three parties of men scattered over thousands of miles of Antarctica to bring home.

Worsley quickly collected the three men left on the south side of South Georgia. The rescue of the party left at Elephant Island was not accomplished quite so smoothly. The whaler *Southern Sky* had sailed directly from Stromness towards Elephant Island with Shackleton on board, but she was blocked by ice and retreated to Port Stanley in the Falkland Islands. The same difficulty befell *Instituto de Pesca No.1*. A third attempt was made in SY *Emma* from Punta Arenas and again ice prevented the ship from approaching the marooned men, who knew nothing of the attempts to save them (in fact, they had no idea if Shackleton had even managed to reach South Georgia and raise the alarm). Each attempt took about one month, with Shackleton's anxiety building all the while.

Eventually, the Chilean ship *Yelcho* reached Elephant Island and Shackleton rowed ashore to hear the men shout the best news possible: "All well, Boss!" During their four-month wait they had kept their spirits up with poetry, among other things. Reginald James wrote these lines and Leonard Hussey added music with his banjo, in praise of the men's leader on the island, Frank Wild:

My name is Frankie Wild-o.
Me hut's on Elephant Isle.
The wall's without a single brick

And the roof's without a tile.
Nevertheless I must confess,
By many and many a mile,
It's the most palatial dwelling place
You'll find on Elephant Isle.

On arrival in Punta Arenas the party enjoyed a wonderful reception and the band moved Shackleton to tears as they played the overture to Franz von Suppé's *The Poet and Peasant*.[134]

Shackleton then hurried around the world to New Zealand to join in the relief of the *Aurora* party from the Ross Sea. The *Aurora* expedition had successfully laid depots towards the South Pole for the *Endurance* team's Antarctic crossing, which never transpired. This achievement had come at the cost of three lives, two lost needlessly, the third due to illness. Arnold Spencer-Smith died first from scurvy, while Aeneas Mackintosh and Victor Hayward set out over sea ice that the rest of the party considered to be unstable and were never seen again. All three deaths weighed very heavily on Shackleton. He was physically and emotionally exhausted when he returned to a Britain at war.

Shackleton believed that "To take part in this war... is a matter of saving... a man's own opinion of himself."[135] That his self-opinion needed saving was in part a reaction to the failure of the *Endurance* expedition and in particular the lack of confidence in him demonstrated by the *Aurora* Relief Committee with their decision not to give him command of the expedition to save his own men of the Ross Sea party. He was seeking to set these wrongs right and to regain confidence through "the everlasting glory and exaltation of war."[136] The generation who lived through the Great War would often categorize their men as either having had a good or bad war. This was on the basis of action seen; to have had a good war meant to have faced the enemy. Shackleton was destined, to his disappointment, to have a bad war.

War poetry did not seem to engage or interest Shackleton. In part, this was perhaps due to his isolation from world affairs over the preceding two years. Like an audience member joining at the interval, he had missed act one and with it the slow build-up and nuances of the plot. "We were like men arisen from the dead to a world gone mad… to a World-Conflict that had grown beyond all conceptions," he remarked, calling the conflict "the most stupendous war in history"[137]—an appropriate adjective for a war so huge that it is shocking just to contemplate it.

The publication of war poetry did not occur contemporaneously with the action. The earliest works by the best known poets, such as Wilfred Owen, Siegfried Sassoon and Rupert Brooke, were published in late 1916 and many poems and war poets did not see the printed page until after armistice. The way we see the Great War today as a "cultural benchmark" was not shared by those living through the conflict. For example, it was not until the "1970s and 1980s [that Wilfred] Owen was established as the defining poetic voice of the Great War in the English speaking world."[138]

Indeed, Shackleton's enjoyment of poetry appears to have waned during the First World War. The period is associated with a resurgence in the popularity and potency of the medium but Shackleton makes no mention of the war poets. Having a "bad war" meant that he would have been keen to move on. He is unlikely to have had anything more than a passing interest in the powerfully reflective verses of Brooke, Sassoon *et al.* Of his favourite poets only one contributed war poetry: Robert Service (who worked as a war correspondent and ambulance driver)— and even he does not get a mention.

During the war Shackleton realized that the gravity of the geo-political situation far exceeded that of his own adventures and imaginings. To paraphrase H. G. Wells' *Anticipations*, war will become less a question of dramatic short scuffles but ever more monstrous. Ever a fighter, he may have felt a sense of guilt that for the first two years of the conflict he had been hidden from (or worse, could be accused of deliberately hiding from) a "world darkened by desperate strife."[139]

The Great War "is remembered through poetry, not prose.

All British papers carried reams of facts... but of the reality of this most terrible of wars, the horror and the stink, the blood and the misery, very little appeared. Official censorship was part of the reason."[140] This censorship was part of a larger programme of propaganda, a programme which engaged poets and Shackleton too.

Modern propaganda techniques were first used by opposing combatants in the 1914-18 conflict. A War Propaganda Bureau was established soon after the start of the war and was charged with producing materials to persuade men to join up and foreign nations to join the Allies. The bureau employed a number of Shackleton's favourite poets and writers, including Rudyard Kipling, G. K. Chesterton and Gerald Gould. The secretive and compartmentalized nature of this work probably meant that Shackleton did not know that he was working within the same team as many of his literary heroes.

Shackleton was dispatched to South America, in order to assess the effectiveness of the Allied propaganda campaign. He threw himself into the work wholeheartedly and, just as when appointed to RSGS, he found that he had taken the project as far forward as possible within just six months. He was recalled to London, tailed en route by a spy who was arrested when their ship put into New York. This brush with espionage would have thrilled Shackleton, and his next posting combined secrets with exploration.

Spitsbergen, a group of islands roughly half way between the top of Norway and the North Pole, was a strategically located no-man's-land in the Arctic. Here the Germans had created a foothold and established a weather station. Shackleton's task was to join forces with Frank Wild and a genuine but rather secretive mining organization called the Northern Exploration Company. Under the guise of geological exploration they were to maintain a British presence on the islands and keep an eye on the Germans.

Shackleton never made it to Spitsbergen although he did make it across the Arctic Circle. At Tromsø he was recalled to

In uniform at last: Major Shackleton heads to northern Russia
(Wikimedia Commons)

London and given a new mission (Frank Wild again stood in for the absent Shackleton and continued to Spitsbergen). This time, Shackleton's task was to complete the designing and procurement of equipment required for the winter campaign of the North Russian Expeditionary Force. Shackleton was buoyed by the challenge of a new assignment, which came with the rank of Major and a uniform; at last he felt he was participating in the war. He revelled in the time pressure, with only six weeks to prepare before he was to sail to Murmansk. Soon he was happily back in the Polar Regions and with a worthwhile job to do, so his thoughts were able to turn again to a little poetry. He wrote to his son Raymond:

> We are now up in the cold weather, but it is clear and fine, and
> at night there is a wonderful aurora swinging across the sky. The
> moon lies low on the horizon, and circles the head of the world. You
> could write a poem of all the glory of this wonderful North.[141]

If Shackleton himself wrote such a poem then it has not survived. Raymond had written a number of verses, and his father encouraged him:

> I want you to send me copies of any that you have written; and do
> keep it up, for the love of poetry is good, no matter whether one's
> life is carried on at home or in the wild places of the world.[142]

A small number of Raymond's poems do survive, focusing on the rural beauty of Britain but none evokes the wilder places of the world as his father's do.

One recipient of Shackleton's clothing procurement and supply activities in Russia was an American serviceman who wrote about it in verse. Surprisingly, despite all of his polar experience, it appears that the Shackleton boots were not quite right for the icy conditions:

> *Ode on the Shackleton Boot...*
> *...by one who tackled it*

I am the guy I'm the giddy gallot
Who tried to dance in the Shackleton boot
Out of the house and into the street
I find it not easy to keep on my feet
One step forward and two steps back
A side slip and down with a hell of a thwack
Up like a fairy and forward I shoot
All on account of the Shackleton boot.[143]

At Murmansk, Shackleton met a man called Captain Birch-Jones when he was out skiing one day. Surveying a desolate landscape around the base, Shackleton quoted Browning, most likely a passage from "Childe Roland to the Dark Tower Came", which contains many images of lifeless level landscapes, such as:

I think I never saw
Such starv'd ignoble nature: nothing throve

The fellow officer had been reading English at university before he was called up and recognized the quotation as Browning. Shackleton was surprised and declared that Birch-Jones was the "First man in... uniform I've met who'd even heard of Robert Browning". Shackleton later flummoxed him with another quotation as Birch-Jones recalled:

"I don't know who said that."

"Well, Shackleton said it" [replied Shackleton].
"That explorer-man?" I asked, "he must have been a man of parts. I never knew he was a poet!"
Again he turned on me. "Then why the devil did you think he became an explorer?"

I can't remember when my eyes were more completely opened.[144]

Shackleton's vehement reply is a perfect illustration of how he saw himself as a poet-explorer. The poetry came first and exploration was simply its natural consequence.

*

Some of the Shackleton poetic spark was returning towards the end of his time in Russia. At the end of the war he stayed on in Russia, eventually resigning his commission in February 1919 with a sense that while his job in the north was done he had not really played a part in the war, certainly not a fighting role. He dedicated his book *South* "To my comrades who fell in the white warfare of the South and on the red fields of France and Flanders," which reveals where Shackleton, subconsciously at least, thought the real war was fought. In fact, of his comrades on *Endurance* only two died in the war and neither was in France or Flanders. Alfred Cheetham was killed in action in the North Sea and Timothy McCarthy was torpedoed in the English Channel. I doubt that Shackleton intended to snub their memory.

On returning home, to complete work on the manuscript of *South* and to attempt to earn a living through lecturing, Shackleton was decidedly detached from the society around him. The world had changed and his mood was the opposite of that in the nation he returned to. Britain was victorious and optimistic, while he was low: "In the midst of the luxury and excitement of London, Shackleton was harder put to it than ever..."[145] Several elements coalesced to produce this feeling, which had been rumbling since the return of the *Nimrod* expedition in 1909. The problem was that Shackleton had never quite made it to the finish line. He had been 97 miles short in 1909, did not even start the crossing of Antarctica in 1914 and never fired a shot during the war. While his expedition exploits had been outstanding, the war had created a new kind of hero. People of that time might well ask, "Who was Shackleton?" The family finances played a part too. He deployed his usual remedy to all ills, and set about making plans for another expedition. Emily wrote that "it was chiefly his liabilities that made him go this last time..."[146]

14 QUEST

Shackleton's last expedition to Antarctica on M/S *Quest* stands out for its lack of ambition or clear goal. He joined again with his old comrades. A photograph showing Wild and Shackleton sitting on deck enjoying a yarn accurately depicts the atmosphere on board. It was a time of comfort, reminiscence, anecdotes and a feeling of what might have been—"what if".

"If", appropriately, was a permanent fixture onboard *Quest* because Shackleton had commissioned the verses of Rudyard Kipling's poem to be engraved onto a series of brass plaques, which were affixed on the bridge. This poem encourages calm amidst calamity and clearly it meant a great deal to Shackleton. While the lines were important on *Quest*, they were essential motivation six years before. "If" had hung in a frame on the wall of his cabin on board *Endurance*. It was one of the few items that he saved from the ship as she went down in the Weddell Sea and he kept it with him as he made his way around the globe in October 1916 to recover the men of the *Aurora* party from the Ross Sea.

Shackleton had found the end of 1916 a trying time. There were difficulties with the Relief Committee of the expedition, and the fact that he was not in command of it. He wrote, "I am anxious more and more to see our 10 men safe and well and then I will rest."[147] Shackleton obviously felt that the New Year of 1917 began in a more positive fashion than the old year had ended. As the relief ship sailed south, they had to negotiate the belt of pack-ice which bars the passage to the Ross Sea. On occasions this ice barrier can take days or weeks to cross but Captain John King Davis navigated to the open water beyond the ice in just a few hours. Shackleton was relieved and hastily manufactured a New

Year's card for Davis from the cherished poem:

> These lines hung in my cabin throughout the Endurance's voyage and were with me on the floe. I now hand them to you on this first day of a New year which I trust may be of certainty successful as its dawn promises.

He had underlined the words

> And so hold on when there is nothing in you
> Except the will that says to them "Hold on!"

no doubt more as a message to himself than for Davis.

Among the poets in Shackleton's library, Kipling sat somewhere closest to Robert Service, and quite different from Browning and Tennyson. Kipling's style is summed up in the title of two of his volumes of poetry called *Barrack-Room Ballads*. For Shackleton, these were suitable ward room ballads, both entertaining and instructive.

Rudyard Kipling's background was as colourful as Shackleton's; he was well travelled and had his own share of scrapes and controversy. Shortly after his marriage in 1892, Kipling had settled in the American state of Vermont. A public row then erupted with his in-laws which snowballed through press speculation and ended in court proceedings. Kipling's wife Carrie noted that "these are dark days for us". The Kiplings left Vermont in 1896 and slipped suddenly and quietly back to England.

It became the Kipling family habit to spend part of each summer in South Africa, and it was here that Shackleton and Kipling first met. While shipping troops to Cape Town on *Tintagel Castle* in March 1900, Shackleton spied his poetic hero leaning over the rail of another ship in port and hurried across the dockside, eager meet him. Shackleton was received cordially and, taking advantage of the opportunity, asked if Kipling would contribute a verse as a foreword to the book of their voyage.

Rudyard Kipling, whose verse "If" meant so much to Shackleton
(Bonhams/Wikimedia Commons)

Shackleton shared the role of editor with William Maclean for the book *"O.H.M.S." An illustrated record of the voyage of S.S. "Tintagel Castle" ... from Southampton to Cape Town, March, 1900.* It was more a souvenir magazine of the troop-carrying voyage than a book and there were contributions from troops and officers alike. Recounting the scenes as the ship departed from port, Shackleton diverged from his newspaper style and described a lady ashore: "her lips are tightly shut, for should she try to speak 'twould be a sob—and she cares so much. To paraphrase Kingsley 'Men must fight and women must weep.'" Charles Kingsley was a priest, historian and writer; he died in 1875. The line which Shackleton misquotes is from the poem "The Three Fishers" (1851), no doubt remembered from his childhood. As a young man, Shackleton followed Kingsley's example by abstaining from alcohol.

The book included descriptions of light moments of the voyage such as the Crossing of the Line Ceremony at the equator which occasioned some home-spun poetry, but none of the rhymes are Shackleton's. In many ways, *"O.H.M.S."* was a forerunner to *The South Polar Times* and *Aurora Australis*, but unlike the Antarctic publications it fails to convey much of the atmosphere of the voyage. Emily later commented that "It is very lightly written, and shows none of the genius, which I find in 'South'!"[148]

Kipling politely agreed to provide the forward for *"O.H.M.S."*, but it was never forthcoming. This did not prevent the two men becoming acquainted later in life. In between expeditions Shackleton and Wild were entertained to lunch at Batemans, Kiping's family home in Sussex, on 8 June 1914.

*

"If" was written about Leander Starr Jameson, a Scottish doctor who in 1878 moved to South Africa, where he became a fixture among Kipling's associates. Like Shackleton he had a magnetic personality and would have been the centre of attention at parties. Even after he led an ill-advised military misadventure against Boer interests, for which he was sentenced to fifteen months in prison, he was still lionized by the press and public. Jameson bounced back, became a politician and was for a short time Prime Minister of the Cape Colonies. Shackleton left no written opinion about Jameson, but I am sure he would have admired Jameson's style. "If" was written during the early part of 1910, following a visit by Jameson to Batemans the preceding October, as advice to Kipling's son John.

IF

IF you can keep your head when all about you
Are losing theirs and blaming it on you,
If you can trust yourself when all men doubt you,
But make allowance for their doubting too;
If you can wait and not be tired by waiting,
Or being lied about, don't deal in lies,
Or being hated, don't give way to hating,
And yet don't look too good, nor talk too wise:

If you can dream - and not make dreams your master;
If you can think - and not make thoughts your aim;
If you can meet with Triumph and Disaster
And treat those two impostors just the same;
If you can bear to hear the truth you've spoken
Twisted by knaves to make a trap for fools,
Or watch the things you gave your life to, broken,
And stoop and build 'em up with worn-out tools:

If you can make one heap of all your winnings
And risk it on one turn of pitch-and-toss,
And lose, and start again at your beginnings
And never breathe a word about your loss;
If you can force your heart and nerve and sinew
To serve your turn long after they are gone,
And so hold on when there is nothing in you
Except the Will which says to them: 'Hold on!

If you can talk with crowds and keep your virtue,

Or walk with Kings - nor lose the common touch
If neither foes nor loving friends can hurt you,
If all men count with you, but none too much;
If you can fill the unforgiving minute
With sixty seconds' worth of distance run,
Yours is the Earth and everything that's in it,
And - which is more – you'll be a Man, my son!

*

In the years prior to the voyage of *Quest*, Shackleton was marking time. Back in 1900, joining Scott's *Discovery* expedition was a chance to "break away from the monotony of method and routine."[149] Now in 1919 he was engaged in the depressingly routine and novelty-lacking business of lecturing to make a living. Every day for months on end he talked to half-full halls of post-war audiences.

The First World War had brought down the curtain on the heroic age of Antarctic exploration. The pole had been conquered but the age of aeronautical exploration and concept of "Antarctica as a continent for science" were some years away in the future.* The great white field of the south lay fallow for the next ten years; indeed after Scott, the South Pole itself would not be visited for another forty years.

At first, the *Quest* expedition was conceived to journey north, not south, with the aim of discovering new lands in the vast area to the north of Canada's North-West Territories (known today as Nunavut). Vihjalmur Stefansson had accomplished just such a feat in the Beaufort Sea only a few years previously. Shackleton sought help from the Canadian government to expand the boundaries of the dominion still further; an old school friend John Quiller Rowett promised part of the funding.

---

* Immediately after Tryggve Gran's return from the *Terra Nova* expedition, Shackleton discussed the possibility of taking an aeroplane to Antarctica with him. Although that plan came to naught, Gran went on to become the first man to fly across the North Sea.

Perhaps Rowett hoped to be rewarded with his name on the map, but his writings suggest that his motive was purely altruistic. He had money and lots of it, while Shackleton did not. "The expedition cost me a great deal more than I intended," he wrote in 1922, but "I shall always be grateful for the friendship we had for each other."[150] This was just as well because at the last minute the Canadian government support for the expedition failed to materialize. So it was that Shackleton put the helm hard over and set the course to familiar grounds in the south in a venture known officially as the British Oceanographic and Subantarctic Expedition.

The *Quest* expedition was not a happy time for Shackleton. His previous expeditions had been optimistically led and joyously driven conscious choices to voyage *towards* the uttermost. The voyage of *Quest* had more to do with sailing *away* and leaving troubles behind. Just before the departure of the *Quest*, Shackleton wrote a magazine article (it was never published, as far as I can tell). The article explains the value of polar exploration, but it is a dull and workmanlike essay, devoid of poetry or rhetoric.[151] Shackleton felt that sailing away on another adventure was the only thing he could do. A former, office-based colleague wrote, "he was the first to admit, with that big laugh of his which one never forgets, that office work was out of his line altogether."[152] Expeditioning was the only thing he was really good at, so he had no real alternative but to do one more.

Shackleton must have known that this would be his last trip to the Antarctic, and it was time to reinvent himself. But first the *Quest* expedition, filled with familiar shipmates and destined for old stomping grounds, provided a temporary escape. For Shackleton as poet and thinker, time at sea was always his most productive. He cherished the opportunity to let his imagination work under the stars, the same stars that had inspired him and barred the way to temptations of the flesh in his merchant marine days.

He would have envied Kipling's writing methods. The sea

days were a productive time for him too. Kipling used to set up a card table on deck and, oblivious to the bustle around about him, he would settle down and write. Kipling, of course, had the advantage that he was always travelling for pleasure: there were no such luxuries for the working Shackleton.

On board *Quest*, Shackleton's muse returned and he parodied a verse of "If". His version shows how, having escaped from England, his mood improved and once again he was in his element, enjoying the company of old friends and a few suitably selected new sailing companions. Scribbled in his own hand on a piece of card, the poem is complete with mistakes and deletions. On the reverse of the card are five photographs of his shipmates at Madeira. True to form, it is likely that the verse would have been read aloud for all to enjoy at a mess dinner.

IF

If you can stand the Quest and all her antics
When all around you turn somersaults upon her deck;
And go aloft when no one has told you
And not fall down and break your blooming neck;
If you can work like Wild and also like Wuzzles
Spend a convivial night with some old bean,
And then come down and meet the Boss at breakfast
And never breathe a word of where you've been.
If you can fill the port and starboard bunkers
With fourteen tons of coal; and call it fun;
Yours is the ship and everything that's in it
And you're a marvel; not a man my son.[153]

"Wuzzles" was the nick name given to Frank Worsley, captain of *Endurance*, navigator of the *James Caird* and now commanding *Quest*. "All her antics" refers to the general un-seaworthiness of the vessel. The smallest of all of Shackleton's expedition ships, *Quest* was ideal for the relatively sheltered waters of the Canadian Arctic but, with the enforced change of plans, she was ill-suited to the long ocean passages required to sail south. Two sailors had to be sent home from Lisbon due to the effects of continuous sea-sickness. The note about the bunkers is praise for the expedition scientists who were not able to do any real work on the early part of the voyage because they were always being called upon to move coal.

*

Today Ernest Shackleton is held up as a model of good management style, and it is true that when on expedition he put the men's interests first. It is perhaps strange, then, that barring the mention of Wild and Wuzzles above, that of all the loyal companions who served with him in trying situations the only individual to merit his own poem was Gerald Lysaght. Lysaght joined *Quest* from Plymouth to Madeira in 1921 and is relatively unknown in the Shackleton story.

Shackleton and Lysaght had both been passengers on SS *India* when Shackleton travelled south to join *Nimrod* in 1907. Lysaght took an interest in the expedition and "wrote a poem on it which he copied into a book of his verses which he gave to Shackleton."[154] (Unfortunately I have not been able to find a book of verses by Lysaght, either with or without a handwritten verse.) They became friends and Lysaght introduced Shackleton to the poems of George Meredith. Lysaght made his fortune in the steel industry and gave financial support to the *Nimrod* expedition. He was rewarded with a mountain named after him. Years later, Shackleton invited him to join in a part of the voyage of *Quest*. Shackleton wrote these lines as a farewell present for Lysaght when he prepared to leave the ship at Cape Verde, having stayed on board much longer than originally planned. Shackleton valued the advice, friendship and loyalty of all of those who supported him, even those who remained in the background.

To Gerald Lysaght, A.B.

After these happy days, spent in the oceanways,

Homeward you turn!
Ere our last rope slipped the quay and we made for the open sea
You became one of us.
You have seen the force of the gale fierce as a thresher's flail
Beat the sea white;
You have watched our reeling spars sweep past the steady stars
In the storm-wracked night.
You saw great liners turn; high bows that seemed to churn
The swell we wallowed in;
They veered from their ordered ways, from the need of time-kept
days,
To speed us on.
Did envy possess your soul; that they were sure of their goal
Never a damn cared you,
For you are one with the sea - in its joy and misery
You follow its lure.
In the peace of the Chapel Cleeve, surely you must believe,
Though far off from us,
That wherever the Quest may go; what winds blow high or low –
Zephyrs or icy gale;
Safe in our hearts you stand; one with our little band.
A seaman, Gerald, are you!

After Cape Verde, *Quest* lurched and wallowed to Rio de Janeiro before the final leg of her voyage to Antarctica in the last months of 1921.

15 "PROSPICE"

Robert Browning and Ernest Shackleton shared a dislike of school. Neither man flourished until he found his true vocation. For Browning, this was to be his writing life in Florence, Italy. Browning described his time there as his university, in much the same way as Shackleton learnt more at sea than he ever had at school. Both men depended on their wife's inherited wealth to keep them, which at the time would have come with a certain stigma. Both fought for position throughout their whole lives. Although they were recognized during the early parts of their respective careers, Browning only achieved literary acclaim during the last years of his life and Shackleton's reputation reached its peak in the 1980s, some sixty years after his death.

In a 1910 interview for *The Captain,* a paper for boys, Shackleton identified why he enjoyed Browning's works: "I greatly love and admire Browning. He is a fine spirit. I like his optimism, his note of 'Never say die', the grand way in which he faces the future, his outlook upon the world. Yes I think Browning is great."[155]

Much of Browning's poetry takes the form of monologue during which the protagonist attempts to justify and explain past actions, seeking acquittal from the reader who sits as jurist. "Prospice" is unusual because Browning wrote as himself. As a result its themes are arguably clearer than in some of his other works.

Shackleton and Browning both seemed to have been drawn to unorthodox characters, for example Paracelsus who was an unsavoury but effective sixteenth-century physician. A review of Browning's works that appeared in *The Times* in 1880 described them as "obscure" and having a "seductive raciness".[156] Shackleton

Herbert Rose Barraud's c1888 photograph of Robert Browning, of whom Shackleton said "No poet ever met the riddle of the universe with a more radiant answer" (Wikimedia Commons)

wrote that "it must be remembered that the men whose desires lead them to the untrodden paths of the world have generally marked individuality". Another contemporary reviewer stated that Browning "requires some amount of study... But it will repay all the trouble bestowed upon it."[157] Ernest and Emily certainly took that trouble and were repaid with a poet's insight which provided them with a valuable form of intellectual and moral guidance for their marriage and life.

Shackleton summarized his love of Browning thus:

> I tell you what I find in Browning is a consistent, a spontaneous optimism... No poet ever met the riddle of the universe with a more radiant answer. He knows what the universe expects of man— courage, endurance, faith—faith in the goodness of existence.[158]

*

"Prospice", meaning "forward looking", is referred to at many points throughout Ernest Shackleton's adult life and was particularly significant for him and Emily.

Polar exploration at the beginning of the twentieth century was a hazardous way to make a living. In the words of the apocryphal advertisement, "safe return doubtful".* With this choice of poem Ernest was preparing Emily to face the future, whatever that might be.

Robert Browning wrote "Prospice" a few weeks after the death of his wife, Elizabeth Barrett Browning, from the tuberculosis which had afflicted her since before their wedding. Written by a husband following the death of his spouse, it is easy to see how it felt relevant to Ernest and Emily as they contemplated "the worst", hoped for "the best" and determined to be brave.

---

* The full text of the mythical advertisement for the *Endurance* expedition runs: "Men wanted for hazardous journey, small wages, bitter cold, long months of complete darkness, constant danger, safe return doubtful, honor and recognition in case of success." The "original" has never been found and it is likely that it never existed.

According to "Prospice", death itself would bring both reunion and rest. This must have been of enormous comfort, particularly to Emily who wrote: "'Prospice' became our watchword, he always used it telegrams up to the last one he sent—'Prospice'! means just everything, if only it is the truth..."[159]

Prospice

Fear death? - to feel the fog in my throat,
The mist in my face,
When the snows begin, and the blasts denote
I am nearing the place,
The power of the night, the press of the storm,
The post of the foe;
Where he stands, the Arch Fear in a visible form,

Yet the strong man must go:
For the journey is done and the summit attained,
And the barriers fall,
Though a battle's to fight ere the guerdon be gained,
The reward of it all.
I was ever a fighter, so - one fight more,
The best and the last!
I would hate that death bandaged my eyes, and forbore,
And made me creep past.
No! let me taste the whole of it, fare like my peers,
The heroes of old,
Bear the brunt, in a minute pay glad life's arrears
Of pain, darkness and cold.
For sudden the worst turns the best to the brave.
The black minute's at end,
And the elements' rage, the fiend-voices that rave,
Shall dwindle, shall blend,
Shall change, shall become first a peace out of pain.
Then a light, then thy breast,
O thou soul of my soul! I shall clasp thee again,
And with God be the rest!

The direct question at the beginning suggests that some criticism is being answered. This criticism comes from within; that to approach death with "bandaged eyes" or, worse still, to "creep past" would be to take a cowardly route. It exposes an implicit fear of death which must be suppressed, or better still conquered. The question is answered resoundingly with a "No!" How appropriate for a polar explorer that it should be snowy blasts that announce he is reaching "the place". However a mystery remains: is this the place of reunion or of death?

For Shackleton "life's arrears" could only have meant his constant debts and "the reward of it all" would have been that far-off dream of financial security. Debts were a constant millstone and, according to Emily, the main reason he continued to return to Antarctica. Shackleton also endured a good deal of criticism, in particular from the learned societies such as the Royal Geographical Society, and he may well have looked forward to a dwindling of the "fiend voices that rave".

*

Sitting in Torquay in the summer of 1907 while holidaying with the children, Emily Shackleton wrote a note for her husband who was busy preparing for the *Nimrod* expedition. The note was to be opened on Midwinter's Day one year hence. For Antarcticans, Midwinter's Day is the primary "feast day" of the year. It is still kept as such today, in preference to Christmas Day which occurs in the middle of the busy summer sledging season. Emily wrote: "for the darkness will be half over and you will be looking forward to achievements [;] achieve much! ... Of this be certain though: that if you don't do all, or half, or a quarter of what you hope to do it will make no difference to me darling."[160]

This letter could be interpreted as expressing a lack of confidence in her husband's abilities, or even a loss of faith in the expedition; but it also indicates that for Emily, Shackleton's safe return was more important than reaching any pole. She reassured him of this when he did return and asked her whether a live donkey was better than a dead lion.

Emily entrusted her letter to Eric Marshall, to be given to Shackleton on 21 June 1908. Without realizing it, Shackleton replied to the missive eight months before he opened it. Writing to Emily in October 1907 he said, "I will come back to you safe and well" and "I will take every care and run no risks."[161]

*

When my own wife read these words from Ernest to Emily, her immediate response was to shout out "liar!", and Emily must have known this too. No true expedition is without risk and the *Nimrod* expedition was no exception. It was only luck which brought Shackleton home as a "live donkey", having stretched and stretched the men's daily rations on the journey—and just scraped back.

In contrast, Kathleen Scott sent her husband south with a very different message. Kathleen understood Scott's drive for the South Pole and his keen sense of duty to his country. He had demonstrated these traits on the *Discovery* expedition, before they had even met. She also knew that Scott was a worrier. Like Shackleton, Scott felt a very strong sense of duty and love for his wife and their young son Peter. Kathleen returned this love fiercely and she felt her role was to do everything in her power to support Scott in his chosen endeavour. To ensure that he would not have to face the potentially disabling dilemma of choosing between twin loyalties of home and country, Kathleen wrote him a brave and selfless letter, instructing her husband to act as he would have done before he had met her or Peter:

> …when you are away south I want you to be sure that if there be a risk to take or leave you will take it, or if there is a danger for you or another man to face, it will be you who face it, just as much as before you met Doodles [Peter] and me.

Scott took these powerful words with him to the pole and the letter was recovered after his death along with his diaries and a photograph of his wife and child. The words have lost none of their potency one hundred years on.

Thus Kathleen, with love, had given her permission for Scott to march on until death—if he considered it to be for the best. Emily did not give Shackleton that permission.

*

In Shackleton's mind, safe return was never in doubt. While he had life in him, he would be fighting to get home in order to enjoy the rewards of his journey. His goal in exploration was not the selfless discoveries of new lands for the benefit of mankind, but rather the fame and status such discoveries would bring him. He set out to make a name for himself. Naturally the planting of the Union Flag on the pole and returning with a trophy photograph were intrinsic to this aim. But without returning *alive*, all this effort would be pointless.

Despite the theme of "Prospice" being reunion after death, Shackleton certainly looked forward to seeing Emily again *antemortem*. Ever the optimist, he focused on positive and inspiring poetic pieces to sustain him through trials and it is these phrases that crop up throughout his personal writings—at the expense of any notion of mortality. Uppermost in his mind and writings were

> - one fight more,
> The best and the last!

and

> For sudden the worst turns the best to the brave...

Even so, expeditioning is a dangerous business, and "Prospice" articulated for both Ernest and Emily their mutual understanding that, should the worst happen, they would meet again at the end. Emily explained, "we used it in telegrams as a code, to breathe courage when parted and the hope of reunion". And after Shackleton's death she wrote: "The last two lines gave me hope in the darkest days of loneliness and they are still to me like a beckoning hand."[162]

*

In the National Maritime Museum at Greenwich I discovered a remnant of Shackleton's library. Complete with a Shackleton bookplate and his signature on the first page, is a volume of *The Poetical Works of Robert Browning*.[163] The binding is in good condition and I doubt if the book has been on an expedition. To be able to hold this book, previously thumbed by Shackleton and Emily, is a huge thrill. Not only is it their book, but it contains their annotations and underlining of passages of particular significance.

Turning to "Prospice", it was a real pleasure to see that he had taken a pencil and underlined the same last sentence that Emily referred to as a beckoning hand:

> O thou soul of my soul! I shall clasp thee again,
> And with God be the rest!

When it came, Shackleton's own death was over "in a minute". He died suddenly, from a heart attack. Although he had been under the weather in the weeks before, this malaise was mostly due to the pressures of the *Quest* expedition and sailing through southern ocean storms. His own "black minute" was a quick end, in his cabin at anchor in South Georgia.

16 SHACKLETON'S LAST VERSE

I sat at a table in the archives of the Scott Polar Research Institute where treasures were delivered to me enveloped in identical A3-size plastic wallets. Large-type instructions adorned the front: "Use only pencil for taking notes. Wash your hands before touching the documents." I signed the receipt and was then allowed to open the wallet. At this point SPRI MS 1537/3/9 is revealed to be a beautiful, red leather-bound book. Its cushioned covers are held closed by a brass clasp. No inscriptions or titles are printed on the outside. It shines, brand new, yet it is almost a hundred years old. The smudges, dog-eared pages and water stains that usually accompany an explorer's diary are missing. This is Shackleton's last diary and it only contains entries for the first four days of 1922, each written in the clean comfort of his cabin onboard *Quest*.

Quest had left Rio de Janeiro, bound for South Georgia, on 18 December 1921. Shackleton took the chance to write some last letters home to friends and family. Among them, this brief note to Rowett, the expedition sponsor, encapsulates Shackleton's mood and character beautifully:

SY Quest, Rio, Dec 18 1921

My Dear John
One hundred and ten degrees in the shade! All the work is done, and we are going. The next you will hear will be, please God, success. Should anything happen in the ice it will have nothing to do with anything wrong with the ship. The ship is all right...

Never for me the lowered banner,
Never the lost endeavour!

Your friend,
Ernest.[164]

He hated the heat as it did nothing to improve his fickle and now failing health. While ill in body, Shackleton remained buoyant as he enjoyed the wonderful and addictive feeling that accompanied the casting off of the lines: anything left undone would remain undone and he would be on his mettle to cope. His optimism shines through with a little white lie about the state of the ship, as she was not to prove so "right". Finally, the fanfare: he was so pleased to be back at his work of exploration that he let out a cheer in a burst of poetry. The lines, slightly misquoted, come from the poem "Cor Cordium" by Fiona Macleod (the penname of William Sharp, 1855-1905).

> Sweet Heart, true heart, strong heart, star of my life, oh, never
> For thee the lowered banner, the lost endeavour!
> The weapons are still unforged that thee and me shall dissever,
> For I in thy heart have dwelling, and thou hast in mine for ever.
>
> Can a silken cord strangle love, or a steel sword sever?
> Or be as a bruised reed, the flow'r of joy for ever?
> Love is a beautiful dream, a deathless endeavour.
> And for thee the lowered banner, O Sweet Heart never!

They follow his characteristic taste for stirring and optimistic poetry that is nonetheless not afraid to contemplate death. Sharp was an enigmatic character, drawn to the occult and a member of the Golden Dawn. Hiding behind a female pseudonym led some biographers to question Sharp's sexuality although he was married. For Shackleton, this unorthodox choice of quotation confirms that his poetic tastes roamed far.

The poem's title (which translates from the Latin as "Heart of Hearts") is shared with a Swinburne verse. Shackleton would have identified with Macleod's allusion of to two hearts cohabiting one inside the other. Just a few weeks previously he had parted painfully from Emily for yet another "last" expedition.

Quest meanwhile was far from being "all right". Just a few days after he had sent the letter to Rowett, Shackleton wrote in his diary: "Things have gone awry: Engines unreliable, furnaces cracked, water short, heavy gales, all that physically can go wrong."[165] Although he claimed that spirits on board were high, it was a sad trip. These latter-day Argonauts were the post-war remnants of the Heroic Age, setting out along the paths less trodden because it was the only thing they knew how to do. With Shackleton came *Endurance* veterans Frank Wild (for his fifth journey south) and Captain Frank Worsley along with McIlroy, Hussey, Green and other familiar names.

Shackleton recognized that the *Quest* expedition was his swan song. He understood, even if he refused to acknowledge it, that he was in poor health. Suffering a southern ocean gale through Christmas would not have helped his mood but he somehow managed to remain upbeat. "There are two points in the adventure of the diver," he wrote on the first day of his new 1922 diary, "One when a beggar he prepares to plunge. One when a prince he rises with his pearl."

In these lines, spoken by the alchemist in the eponymous poem by Browning, Paracelsus sought to justify to his friend Festus his continuing quest for knowledge at the expense of love. In choosing the reference, Shackleton perhaps acknowledged that the cost of his expeditions over the years was the quality of his love for Emily. He had often given Emily second place to his adventures and yet he loved them both. Each expedition was a metaphorical dive from which he hoped to return with the pearl, but the prize was never quite attained and so he had to dive again. Emily once resignedly replied to this line with "while you 'plunge' we 'wait you when you rise'."[166]

In all, 361 pages of the journal are blank. Only the first four days contain pencil written entries. Each entry is in two parts, a melancholy note about the ship or the party's curious sense of death on arrival at the whale processing centre of Grytviken, paired with a poetic, forward-looking note. "I must lead on" appears on 2 January, and on 3 January Shackleton wrote:

> Thankful that I can
> be crossed and thwarted as a man

This is from Browning's epic "Christmas Eve and Easter Day" (the original 1850 publication spanned twenty pages of tightly typed text) that deals with a shaking faith: does God exist? Will Christ rise? Another line from the poem states:

> How very hard it is to be
> A Christian.

At times Shackleton had found it hard to follow the Christian path. Had this poem come to his mind because he knew that he was approaching the end of his life? To be thwarted was to be a man: and being "a man" was his life's aim. While being thwarted might mean to be stopped in one's tracks or scuppered, to Shackleton it meant to be challenged, to be forced to move and therefore to be alive. He always followed his own course, often a hard route where he would thwart and be thwarted. His own way produced results.

Shackleton died in the early hours of 5 January 1922 in his cabin on *Quest* at anchor in Grytviken. His last diary entry, made on the 4 January ends with the words:

> A wonderful evening "In the darkening twilight I saw a lone star
> hover gem like above the bay"

The words in quotation marks seem to be his own, not a quotation. A lone star still hovers above him, carved into his headstone in the cemetery at Grytviken. He is buried around 600 feet from where he died, yet his body crossed the Scotia Sea to South America before coming back to rest. The headstone was set in place six years after his death.

Leonard Hussey, an old *Endurance* shipmate, accompanied

Shackleton's body on the 1,400-mile voyage to Montevideo in Uruguay. There he learnt of Emily's wishes that Shackleton should be buried on South Georgia; so he turned and sailed back south with "the Boss" for the last time. On 5 March 1922 Shackleton was buried in the whalers' graveyard at Grytviken. There are around sixty graves in the cemetery and his stands out. All the others in the neat paddock face, as is traditional, to the east, whereas Shackleton's grave is set at right angles to the others. It is said that he was buried looking towards the south and to Antarctica. If that is the case, then his headstone has been placed on his feet. It is more likely that he is facing north, with his head "pointing" to the south. Either way, even in death, he is going in his own direction.

Shackleton's pale grey granite headstone stands about six feet tall, towering over the simple white painted wooden crosses of the other graves. It is a square-section pillar, made in Scotland and shipped by rail and sea to the South Atlantic. Appropriately enough, it is not finely polished, but well shaped and solid. On the front are carved a ski pole and ice axe, in front of which is depicted a nine-pointed star. Nine, we have seen, was Shackleton's lucky number. It was the ninth day of various months when he first arrived in Antarctica, married Emily, reached his furthest south and so on. Stand behind the stone and one can look out beyond the grave and into the bay where *Quest* and *Endurance* before her lay at anchor. From this position one can read the inscription set in lead letters on the rear of the stone:

> I hold that a man should strive to the uttermost for his life's set prize
> Robert Browning.

Of course, Browning! The lines are from "The Statue and the Bust" and for a man who struggled, whose life was one long quest, it is easy to see how this is a fitting epitaph.

With his head pointing to the south, Shackleton's final resting place at Grytviken, South Georgia (Liam Quinn/Wikimedia Commons)

17 "THE STATUE AND THE BUST"

I hold that a man should strive to the uttermost for his life's set prize.

The story behind these lines makes them more pertinent for Shackleton than anyone might have imagined. They are in fact an oft-repeated Shackletonian misquotation; the original version reads:

Let a man contend to the uttermost
For his life's set prize, be it what it will!

The very next line of Browning's poem, published in 1850, refers to a gamble which did not pay off: "The counter our lovers staked was lost..." The lovers in question are two adulterous Italians struggling to reconcile promises of fidelity made to their spouses with their love for one another—a struggle with which Shackleton would have been familiar. The Duke, the male protagonist of the poem, says

Dear or cheap
As the cost of this cup of bliss may prove
To body or soul, I will drain it deep.

Shackleton too drained deep during his life and ultimately it proved costly; he loved to drink and smoke.* His great granddaughter, Alexandra Shackleton, told me that smoking was more important to him than drinking. Towards the end of his life he complained to his doctors, "What are you trying to get me to give up now?"

---

* Some of the 43 cases of whisky taken on the Nimrod expedition have recently been found intact and the blend recreated. The total amount of spirits ordered for this expedition equated to approximately one bottle per man per week.

The physical strain of successive hauls towards the pole followed by the mental strain of the two-year long *Endurance* saga cannot have contributed to his longevity. Marshall, the doctor on the *Nimrod* expedition in 1907, maintained that Shackleton's heart would not have stood up to the conditions at 13,500 feet on Mount Erebus. Finally, his struggle with faithfulness to his wife created additional stress which no doubt contributed to his early death at forty-seven.

It is widely held that Shackleton had a number of affairs; one of the longest running seems to have been with Rosalind Chetwynd, an American-born actress and actress-manager with whom he shared a business venture.

Affairs can be toxic to a marriage and intoxicating for the participants; no doubt taking a mistress from the stage added an element of piquancy for Shackleton. Rosa Lynd, as she styled herself on stage, was born in the United States as Rosalind Secor. She moved to England and married an heir to a baronetcy, Guy Chetwynd, continuing to use the title Lady Chetwynd after her divorce.

Bridges Adams, a tour manager with the Rosa Lynd Company, was interviewed by Margery and James Fisher by letter for their 1957 biography of Shackleton. Adams was reluctant to make any disclosures in an area where he felt it improper to do so; even today there is a feeling in the theatre business that "what happens on tour remains on tour". In July 1955 he wrote to the Fishers answering a number of questions about the financial and other partnerships between Shackleton and Rosalind. Like many of Shackleton's other business ventures it did not do well and the show closed less than one month after it opened. Adams did not send the letter until March 1956, claiming it to be too "gossipy". Eventually Adams gets around to obliquely confirming the affair with the very last line of the letter: "As to matters into which one mustn't pry: although he was rather fuming at fortune they seemed awfully happy together."[167]

Another infidelity seems to have been with Elspeth Beardmore, the wife of his former employer and expedition sponsor. Elspeth was the antithesis of Rosalind: she was genuinely titled, from the upper class of British society and, with a successful husband, she had no need of work. This affair is revealed by Regina W. Daly's book *The Shackleton Letters*, in which she carefully transcribed a series of letters between Shackleton and Emily on one hand, and Shackleton and Elspeth Beardmore on the other. Daly collected 28 letters spanning more than two years beginning in May 1907 from various archive sources, and presented them in chronological order.

Characteristic of Shackleton's letters to Emily was a wandering nature, frequent abrupt changes in subject and each letter peppered with heartfelt outpourings. By contrast, his early letters to Elspeth are friendly but businesslike. These letters were well structured with each paragraph neatly constraining its subject. That of 6 October 1907 ends as normal with a gentlemanly "Do write a line and tell me how you are". Suddenly there was a marked change and the letter of 15 October, just nine days later, contains an adolescent gush of adoration: "I can see you now standing on the hillside with the wind blowing around you fresh and free with your little slim form and glorious eyes and all that has made *you*."[168]

This second letter to Elspeth is much more in the style of his writings to his wife, and two points stand out. For the first time in a letter to Elspeth, Shackleton wrote about poetry and expressed a wish that they could discuss it together; this was clearly an "Emily and Ernest" activity. Secondly, he referred to Elspeth as "Child" whereas up until then that pet name had been solely reserved for Emily. It appears that a significant change took place in the relationship between Elspeth and Shackleton between the letters of 6 and 15 October 1907.

Shackleton's heartfelt letter of the 15th appears to be replying to a "Dear John" letter from Elspeth. He pleads with her to "never talk about giving me up… about a friendship that is passed… Oh Elspeth dear there is so much more that I want to say," he writes but follows with words not of love or pleading—"to which you can respond"—but with a justification for his departure. His expedition is to be "a feat that will be welcome to you", an echo of his time on the *Discovery* expedition when he set out to achieve great things prior to asking for Emily's hand. He concludes with an extract from "Wander-Thirst" by Gerald Gould,* suggesting that his real focus is his work in the south, and not in continuing the alliance with Elspeth:

> Yonder the long horizon lies, and there by night and day,
> The old ships sail to port again, the young ships sail away,
> And come I may but go I must and if men ask you why,
> You can lay the blame on the stars and sun and the white road and
> the sky.[169]

In any event, Shackleton's pleading was fruitless; Elspeth was effective at cooling the relationship and Shackleton's poor choice of love poetry reduced the potency of the affair. By this time, *Nimrod* had already departed on her voyage south and Ernest was frantically busy in Britain prior to his own departure on 31 October. It is likely that any affair with Elspeth was short-lived; perhaps just one liaison.

The next letters to Elspeth, after a gap of nearly a month during which time Shackleton began his journey south, had returned to friendly cordiality. The only possible reference to any previous liaison was a promise that "your picture will be the one that will reach the Pole".

Of course, the most overt of Shackleton's love affairs was with his mistress Antarctica. Writers often attributed to the continent the female gender; this could simply be because initially "she" only drew male whalers and explorers close. Modern poet Bill

---

* Gerald Gould (1885-1936) wrote a number of popular verses published in newspapers and magazines without achieving any prominence as a poet. Gould worked on propaganda during the First World War, and he went on to edit the novels of George Orwell.

Manhire travelled to Antarctica in 1998, where he visited and was inspired by Shackleton's hut at Cape Royds. He wrote, in a rather breathless and excited style, that "Antarctica is a kind of female body which must be mastered and penetrated by bold, resourceful males. She... is a pure virgin who must be woken gently and warmed into a passionate life."[170] Shackleton expressed the sentiment a little more gently when just before the *Endurance* expedition he wrote to Elspeth "perhaps the Antarctic will make me young again,"[171] clearly hoping that refreshing this love affair would be youth giving. Robert Service referred throughout his writings to the frozen northern lands as female. From Katharine Coles' poem on Antarctica, which is based on Shackleton's favourite verses from the book of Job comes "*Gendered. A woman*".* Antarctica might have warned Emily, in the words of a Robert Service poem: "He was ours before you got him, and we want him once again."

Emily by this time had resigned herself to a role of domestic partner, feeling that she had "failed him somehow". In her letters to Shackleton's biographer, Hugh Mill, she indicated knowledge of the affairs and resignation to the fact, with the rhetorical question, "what else could I have done?"[172]

Was divorce ever on the cards for Ernest and Emily? Shackleton pushed ahead of his time with methods of exploration, while they both enjoyed Browning, who as a poet was ahead of his class. Could they have considered putting themselves ahead of their times and resorting to divorce with the ease that it is accepted today? Such a course of action would not be entertained by either, because despite the affairs and lengthy separations there was a strong bond of love between Emily and Ernest throughout the whole of their lives. Just a few letters after the Elspeth episode, Ernest wrote to Emily: "I made these poor lines

---

* If an exception is required to prove the rule, then in *The Songs of the Morning*, written by Doorly and Morrison, the second officer and chief engineer on *Morning*, a song called "The Ice King" appears. In this hymn to the south, Antarctica is depicted as a male entity and it simply does not ring true.

[,] in places they do not even rhyme well but you will understand a little of what I feel when you read them."

Even Shackleton's best poems are a poor second to those of the great writers he loved. This rhyme is far from his best, as he acknowledges with "My hand in writing falters". Yet it is a home-made love poem, for his "Sweeteyes", with strong echoes of Macleod and Browning. This poem is untitled.

Low in the West is the setting sun,
I am going far from thee
Love of my life my darling,
To the pale and stormy sea
Through nights of tropic flame
Through days of shadow and storm
Heart of my Heart I love you
Darling my own my All.
I want your clinging handclasp
I long for your eyes divine
Wonderful fairness of body
You are mine all mine.
Had I a pen of glory
Could I paint in colours of grace
I would make a wondrous story
Of thy beauty and witching grace.
My hand in writing falters
My eyes grow dim with tears
For long long days are before us
To be filled with hopes and fears.
But again in a joyous meeting
Comes your lover to your breast
Out from the strong endeavour
Seeking the real rest,
There locked in each others arms
Quiet in heart and soul
The weary wandering sailor
Reaches the lovelit goal
Darling my heart I need you
My love will enclose you round
You and our little children
Now lost but then will be found

God keep you all in safety
Away from all storm and strife
You are dearer by far to your husband
Than anything else in life.[173]

Set against the background of the journey ahead but focusing on love and the "joyous meeting" that will end the "long long days [that] are before us" this poem was a much more valuable love token than the lines he borrowed for Elspeth's benefit. Perhaps, having seeing the error of his ways with Elspeth, Ernest was re-committing himself to Emily with the last lines of his own poetic vow. Several phrases are echoes of "Prospice", the verse that symbolizes love and eternity for Emily and Ernest, in particular:

Comes your lover to your breast
Out from the strong endeavour
Seeking the real rest…

Emily loved the letters from Ernest and kept almost all of them, describing them in her correspondence with Mill as "quite wonderful and very beautiful". She singled out the series of which this poem was a part: "There are several very dear ones written in 1907—on his way to N.Z."[174]

✳

The choice of verse for Shackleton's epitaph, calling to mind both unfaithfulness of heart as well as unswerving struggle, can now be seen in a different light. At worst it is damning of the man who lies beneath; at best it is an acknowledgement of the imperfections of his character set against a celebration of his achievements. It was Emily who, having seen and felt the cost of Shackleton's quest for bliss, designed, commissioned and chose the headstone. It is inconceivable that she did not know the overall theme of the poem.

Emily had studied Browning's works at university level and the poem was also the subject of the earliest extant exchange of letters between her and Ernest. In common with many of his letters, he expressed the usual worries about his future prospects, and then got around to poetry. Clearly they had been corresponding about a number of poems and Shackleton was replying to a question from Emily: "The moral of the 'Statue and the Bust'. Surely you know; it is plain true… to me!" And, in a statement reminiscent of Nelson placing the telescope to his blind eye, all Browning's "morbid anatomy" themes are ignored. No mention of the central thrust of the piece, adultery, but instead:

> That a man should strive to the uttermost for his life's set prize. I feel the truth of it but how can I do enough if my uttermost falls short in my perception of what should take the prize…

Back to self-doubt; the young Shackleton saw the path of his life ahead strewn with obstacles. He had put his finger on his life-long problem: his own impossible-to-achieve perception of the deed that would be worthy of the prize.

Through their letters, which span Ernest's adult life, we find more love and life than disappointment and desertion. Their marriage was not perfect, nor was it simple or definable. In the same letter of 1898 Shackleton enclosed a poem for Emily which, unlike Browning's free ranging works, has a singularity of focus, Elizabeth Barrett Browning's "Sonnet 43". This was not only at the start of their relationship, but also the relationship between the young couple and the works of Browning.

Emily always provided Shackleton with a keel with which he could sail the difficult course to windward; but she was never an anchor to him. She would have loved having him at home more often but acknowledged, "One must not chain down an eagle in a barnyard."[175] They had their own version of love and a concept of what marriage should be like. As in Browning's work we find examples of unconventional lifestyles sitting comfortably with strong religious faith, so with the Shackletons' marriage we find a system that would not be to everyone's taste but was founded in a strong mutual love. Elizabeth Barrett Browning's poem explores those elements that made up this marriage: smiles and tears, men striving and feelings so out of sight that they are impossible to write down.

Shackleton, in reply to one of Emily's early letters, finished by suggesting that she was worth more to him than all the poetry in the Browning canon:

> You say you think you could give me something nice to think about in my long night watches: you have.
>
> Now and ever Ernest

For Shackleton is thinking about Emily during those night watches: she had given herself to him.

18 THE LOST POEM

In the Scott Polar Research Institute archives I found a small notebook, bound in a dirty, red fabric cover and containing just six loose leaf pages.[176] A Shackleton poem is written on each page in black ink in very neat handwriting. The handwriting is far too neat to be Shackleton's, although all five poems are his creations:

"L'Envoi", which appears to have been copied from the version in *The South Polar Times* of 1907;
"A Tale of the Sea"—the copier has written in the name Ernest Shackleton underneath, and dated the work February 1895;
"Fanning Isle", with no attribution;
"Erebus", annotated with "by Nemo" and apparently copied from *Aurora Australis*;
"To the Great Barrier", which, like "L'Envoi" appears to have been copied from *The South Polar Times* and with the name Nemo written at the end.

The last poem is initialled "EHS" in Shackleton's own hand. This red book may have been the only attempt during his lifetime to collect the works together. There is no indication of who had gone to such trouble, nor would there be any reason to try to find out, were it not for a mysterious sixth poem.

Alone in its own file among the Shackleton papers at the University of Cambridge is a single sheet of paper.[177] On it a poem is written in the same exceptionally neat hand and black ink but it is unsigned and unattributed. Carefully retained but muddled into the miscellaneous section of the family papers, any record of authorship or provenance has been lost. There are no distinguishing marks on the page, just the title "Until death do us

Join" and eighteen lines of poetry, in two verses:

Until death do us Join

Joy in the stress of the days that used to be!
When Hope and Faith flung out a mesh to reach beyond the sea,
When *he* wrestled with the earth,
Wringing out its hidden worth
And *you* waited safe at home
For the happy time to come
And you both lay down at night to dream of days that were to be.
O the perils of the land, and the perils of the sea,
And the glory of the days that were to be!

Joy in the stress of the days that yet must be!
While Hope and Faith fling out their mesh beyond where the eye
can see,
While *you* wrestle with the earth
Wringing out its hidden worth,
And *he* is safe in harbour, while you toss upon the sea.
There is nothing more to fear,
In the time of exile here,
From the perils of the land and the perils of the sea,
For the glory of the days that are to be!

Without question, the author of the five poems in the red notebook was Shackleton, but what about number six? This verse does not appear in any of his diaries or notebooks, it was not part of *The South Polar Times* or *Aurora Australis* publications, and it is not mentioned by Margery and James Fisher, who in 1957 made the first and only effort to collect Shackleton's poems for publication.[*]

In my weeks of scouring the archives of six different institutions, I had come across one other folder of anonymous poems among the Shackleton papers. Three different verses were included in various hands, one typed. Through the efficiency of *Google*, the author of each poem was quickly identified and

---

[*] Christopher Ralling's book of 1983 simply reprints the appendix from the Fishers' biography containing most of Shackleton's poetry.

over time I was able to find references to these poems within Shackleton's letters, diaries or prose. But put "Until death do us Join" into a search engine and the only match for this corruption of Bishop Cranmer's marriage vows comes from the lyrics to a modern song by the band Séance.[178] *The Columbia Granger's Index to Poetry in Anthologies* produced no results, neither did the British Library.

So in a quest to find the author of the mysterious sixth poem, I began to search for the owner of the exceptionally neat handwriting. Ernest and Emily Shackleton could be ruled out quickly as both had awful handwriting, Emily's even worse than Shackleton's notorious scribble. It is likely that only a member of Shackleton's close family would have had access to all the verses in the red notebook during his lifetime since "A Tale of the Sea" and "Fanning Isle" were not published in any form until after his death. Whoever transcribed the poems was also able to ask Shackleton to authenticate the copy of "To the Great Barrier" with his initials.

Having ruled out Emily, could it have been one of the children: Raymond, Cecily or Edward?

Both Raymond and Edward wrote some poems themselves but the handwriting does not match and the tones of their own poems were significantly different. Raymond's have little literary worth and while Edward's are of better quality, they deal with pastoral themes such as "Poppies in Corn" and the music of evensong wafting over fields.

This left me with Cecily. Alexandra Shackleton, Cecily's niece (and Sir Ernest's granddaughter) suggested that Cecily could possibly have been the transcriber, but with the caveat that she was not literary enough to have been the author.

Only two letters written by Cecily before her father's death survive in the archives to allow a handwriting check. The first was written while Cecily was still at school. She was ten years old when she wrote a note bemoaning the end of term being so far away. Only six lines long, the vast space at the bottom of the page is filled up with many kisses: some large, others small, a row of ten identically sized lined up amongst a random scattering. The handwriting has a childish style but the script is even, letter heights regular, lines run horizontally. If this was the only piece available, we could be no more certain than to describe a match with the poem as a vague possibility.

In the second example, a letter of Christmas Eve 1920 thanking Miss Elizabeth Dawson-Pemberton for her birthday present, the handwriting has tightened considerably. Although not on lined paper it has railway straight precision. There are no blots or splodges of ink, even though she confides in her correspondent that she will have to "wash the ink off my hands because [curiously] my pen is about 1½ inch long..." In particular, the envelope has the closest match of hand: care was required here to ensure correct delivery.

From this example, written when Cecily was fourteen years old, the possibility of a handwriting match with the clear script of the anonymous poem becomes a probability. Perhaps copying out her father's poems was a daughterly distraction on a rainy afternoon. When she proudly presented them to the author, one can imagine Shackleton obliging her wish that he should autograph the last poem in the set.

So if we suppose that Cecily wrote out the poem "Until death do us Join", then the question remains: was she the author of the poem?

We can through the letter mentioned take a look into the world of Cecily Shackleton. "It is a miserable day, raining and blowing" (so an ideal time for the ladylike pursuit of letter writing) while she notes with a hint of disapproval that "[Ray] and Eddie are now playing football outside my room, kicking the paint most of the time". She is looking forward to "this evening [when] Eddie and I are going to a Fancy Dress Ball" and is proud that "Dad is coming afterwards to see us dressed up."[179] I get the feeling that Cecily is quite spoilt. She came home a day earlier than the end of the school term, and makes a point of mentioning it. The purpose of the letter is to thank her aunt for her birthday gift, but this is only slotted in as a "by the way" towards the end.

As likely as it seems that Cecily was the owner of the unusually neat handwriting, there is nothing that conclusively indicates that she was the author of the poem. However, as a witness to her mother and father's fluctuating fortunes in marriage, she may well have written the verses to bolster her widowed mother's spirits and in the hope that in heaven at least they might be able to enjoy a peaceful union. Cecily was sixteen years old when her father died. Certainly old enough to empathize with her mother's grief and the change it must have made to her. The poem is quite sophisticated but well with the capabilities of a sixteen-year-old who has grown up on a diet of poetry from both parents. Certainly Cecily should remain high on the list of suspects.

A number of other clues emerge from a study of the poem. The central theme of a "happy time to come" is one to which Shackleton returns time and again in his letters to Emily. They shared a desire for domestic stability which was never quite achieved because Ernest felt that he had not yet attained his life's set prize, because none of his expeditions had succeeded in their objectives, so he had to venture out again. Yet as we have seen he also revelled in such work: "joy in the stress of the days that used to be". Shackleton often used the word "stress" to mean "busy with work" rather than in the modern accepted meaning of "overloaded with work".

Tennyson in his "Ulysses" discussed the complementary but separate nature of the work of loved ones—in this case a father, who explored, and his son who ruled at home:

He works his work, I mine.

The suggestion in "Until death do us Join" is that while one party has finished work, the other is still busy. Certainly after Ernest's death Lady Shackleton was able to devote more time to her charitable work: for the Browning Settlement and as a Commissioner in the Girl Guide movement. This saw her spend a fair amount of time outdoors although she was not quite "wrestling" with the earth. Could Emily, the poetry scholar, have been the author? I have not found any verses known to be hers, so to test the hypothesis we can do no more than to look at the likely influences on the author.

Barrett Browning concluded her "Sonnet 43" with the suggestion that she may be able to love her husband Robert better still after death. Consider also the conclusion to Robert Browning's "Prospice" where he states that, after death, "O thou soul of my soul! I shall clasp thee again." Did Emily feel that there could be a second chance after the grave?

Reunion through death is a Browning motif; it is the central message of "Prospice", the poem that held so much significance for Ernest and Emily. Death is often linked to freedom or release, and from Swinburne's "The Triumph of Time" comes the line, "Set my soul free as thy soul is free". While the title "Until death do us Join" suggests that one party is dead and the other waiting to join, the verses are more obscure. Is "He wrestled with the earth" a reference to struggling across the Antarctic, or to being dead and buried? The second line of that couplet applies here: does "Wringing out its hidden worth" allude to making a living from the earth, in particular the hidden areas of the globe? The second verse suggests that he is safe in the harbour; is this the harbour of the grave situated in the sheltered cove of Grytviken?

The rhyming scheme and metre of the poem are untidy; this is a feature of many amateur poets so we can draw little conclusion from it. The connection of the words "glory" and "home" is a regular Shackleton trait. The use of the phrase "to be", rather than the more common "to come", as used in relation to a time in the future, also crops up in the Shackleton poem "Erebus". Emily loved, read and re-read his verses, the phrases seeping into her subconscious.

"Until death do us Join" has a peculiar tense structure, for

179

example "to dream of days that were to be". This suggests days (of glory) that could have been achieved but were somehow missed. Such a reflection on bad luck occurs very rarely in Shackleton's writings.

Whilst it would be tempting to claim that this verse, in the same hand as five known Ernest Shackleton, poems was written by Ernest, the theme and tense firmly point to it being written after his death. His other poems all deploy a first-person narrative voice and are clearly set in the present tense or the past. The use of "he" and "you" indicate that a third party wrote the verse.

I have spent much of the last eighteen months dipping in and out of Ernest and Emily's relationship and their tastes in poetry. My conclusion is that this poem was written by someone who not only knew Ernest and Emily well, but also knew their tastes and coping strategies intimately. The use of second- and third-person pronouns is the strongest indicator that the author is Cecily Shackleton. But, considering Alexandra Shackleton's comment that Cecily was not literary enough to write such a supplicated verse, I feel we can not rule out Emily Shackleton. Emily, who formally studied poetry, who shared with Ernest that interest throughout her life has at least equally chance of being the author. She would not be the first poet to write "from the outside" about herself and the first-person pronoun used in the title "Until death do us Join", if it contradicts the body of the work, leaves enough doubt. For the time being this mystery remains unsolved.

19 SHACKLETON'S LEGACY

Ernest Shackleton had the misfortune to see his endeavours eclipsed by the death of Scott and the First World War. It was not until a critical, revisionist biography of Scott written by Roland Huntford was published in 1979 that a fresh look was also taken at Shackleton. As one polar hero was damned, it seems as though we cast about for a replacement.

Shackleton's expeditions and life were re-examined over the subsequent twenty years through books, radio programmes, television documentaries and dramas. I have found six books about Shackleton published before 1979 and stopped counting once I had reached 36 books published since that date. These include children's books, biographies, five "in the steps of" expedition accounts and even the story of Mrs. Chippy, *Endurance*'s cat.

Today it is in the field of leadership and management skills where Shackleton's legacy is felt most strongly (few people remember him for his love of verse). It is his ability to simplify challenges and conundrums to digestible single lines that is attractive to business managers and gurus today. Shackleton used the mission statements and bullet-pointed "core values" beloved of contemporary corporate copywriters before these titles even existed. The reason that he was so skilled with words and turns of phrase was, of course, his lifelong study of poetry.

Shackleton did not merely manage or drive his men; he inspired them, he encouraged them to follow. This is also true of good poetry, whose message is not whipped into us, in which readers are not told what to think. Rather it leads us towards ideas, coaxes us into emotional responses; we are encouraged to follow the poet towards a concept.

Business managers and seminar speakers today choose

Shackleton's aphorisms because, like poetry, his message is enduring. Contemporary celebrities and pop songs may be easier to access but are temporary. Lionel Greenstreet of the *Endurance* expedition said that Shackleton "was always apt in any quotation he made, fitting an occasion or anything that happened".[180] It now seems that leadership teachers can find a Shackleton quotation to suit all business situations. "His work continue[s]... to inspire others around the world," wrote Margot Morrell and Stephanie Capparell in *Shackleton's Way,* the first, and arguably the best book on Shackleton's legacy as a leader.

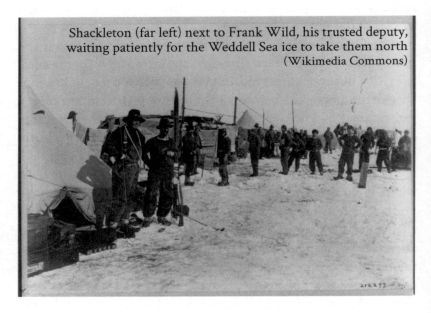

Shackleton (far left) next to Frank Wild, his trusted deputy, waiting patiently for the Weddell Sea ice to take them north (Wikimedia Commons)

Despite the recent examinations of Shackleton's leadership philosophy, the very first book published after his death in 1922 gives the best summary of his personal ideology. To gain that insight the author Harold Begbie talked to Shackleton about poetry.

Begbie rushed to write and publish a book following Shackleton's unexpected death. While it is a slim volume and contains scant details of his expeditions, there are many direct quotations from Shackleton based on interviews Begbie conducted with him over several years for, among other publications the *Daily Telegraph* and the *Children's Encyclopaedia*. Begbie and Shackleton may also have met during the First World War when Begbie's journalism led to propaganda work.

It is a misnomer to call Begbie's volume a biography. Begbie himself entitled the volume *Shackleton: A Memory*, simply Begbie's recollections of numerous meetings with Shackleton collected into "a fuller and more careful sketch" than he could produce in newspaper articles. Lady Shackleton did not approve the publication, but she did not explicitly disapprove of it either. The accuracy of some of Begbie's anecdotes is questionable, which is probably why Mill did not cite him at all and the Fishers caution that Begbie may have been taken in by one or two of Shackleton's taller stories.

Despite these warnings, the passages on poetry ring true. Shackleton used a comparison of two works by Tennyson and Browning on the subject of death to explain his philosophy:

> It seems to me that there are two chief attitudes towards the universe—the attitude you find in Tennyson's Crossing the Bar, beautiful, tender, patient but resigned and certainly passive: and the attitude you find all over Browning.

"Crossing the Bar" was written in 1889. Just before Tennyson died in 1892, he asked his son to ensure that it would always be inserted as the last poem in any publication of his verses.

Crossing the Bar

SUNSET and evening star,
And one clear call for me!
And may there be no moaning of the bar,
When I put out to sea,

But such a tide as moving seems asleep,
Too full for sound and foam,
When that which drew from out the boundless deep

Alfred, Lord Tennyson, whose familiar works Shackleton used to bring the Antarctic alive for audiences at home: portrait by P. Krämer-Friedrich Bruckmann (Wikimedia Commons)

Turns again home.

Twilight and evening bell,
And after that the dark!
And may there be no sadness or farewell,
When I embark;

For though from out our bourne of Time and Place
The flood may bear me far,
I hope to see my Pilot face to face
When I have crost the bar.

Shackleton preferred the way Browning pushed into the tide, and he gave two examples to Begbie, saying: "Take 'Prospice' for example: 'No! let me taste the whole of it, fare like my peers, the heroes of old.' And again in the hackneyed Epilogue to 'Asolando': 'One who never turned back, but marched breast forward'."

It is this positive, forward-looking and occasionally aggressive stance of heroic self-image that has become popular in recent years, particularly with reference to analyzing Shackleton's leadership style.

Shackleton admitted to Begbie that he was annoyed when expeditions were judged simply by what they discovered and put on the map, maintaining that they have a spiritual value. At first glance this may seem a very narrow benefit, accruing only to those who participate in such expeditions, but it is through the honest recollections of the hardships, quarrels, ups and downs of an expedition that wider society can benefit. Poetry goes some way to illuminating those hidden corners of life on the lone trail, corners where dim prose can not penetrate.

*

If Ernest Shackleton has left an unexpected legacy for leadership gurus and writers of sermons, he was not trying to be a pioneer in the field of man-management; it was a natural accident. He has also inspired poets, including among others T. S. Eliot, Bill

Manhire and Katherine Coles. The latter two have benefited from joining Artist and Writers programmes set up by national science bodies, thus continuing the exploration of the spiritual and emotional side of Antarctica.

In the last few years a number of reality television programmes have followed arduous quests in the Polar Regions: races to the South Pole, reconstructions of historic expeditions and celebrity challenges. The focus of these programmes is not on discovery, the environment or science, but on the tears, trials and triumph of the protagonists. Like Shackleton, their participants are bringing the spiritual and emotional side of the expedition to a wider audience.

Shackleton accomplished this through the poets; in Browning he saw an exploration that was far away from the lines of the map: "The bigger the universe, the more [Browning] likes it. He can't feel at home in the longitude and latitude of finity [sic]." We know from Emily that Shackleton brooded on the larger things in life, as she noted, "my husband, who sees the broad lines in everything".[181] The whole picture of creation, and more particularly one's purpose in life, weighed on him. Again for Shackleton, Browning pointed the way:

> No poet ever met the riddle of the universe with a more radiant answer. He knows what the universe expects of man—courage, endurance, faith—faith in the goodness of existence. That's his answer to the riddle.[182]

EPILOGUE

"The explorer is a poet of action, and exploration is the poetry of deeds."
Vilhjalmur Stafannson, Arctic explorer, 1879-1962

Ernest Shackleton would have continued forward to explore the globe and the world of poetry, had he not died so early. No doubt age, maturity and an opportunity for reflection would have improved the quality of his own verse.

During his short life, Shackleton's best poetry *was* his life.

Shackleton embodied the Victorian ideals of manhood and duty. He was able to combine these values with a powerful love, a love of the proportions found in a Browning poem, for Emily. He returned to her every time until the last time, when she who knew him best set his soul free.

Acknowledgements

Thank you to the many people who have helped; I'm sorry if I've missed you off the list. In particular a big thank you to Sarah for constant encouragement, criticism and love.

Hon. Alexandra Shackleton and Jonathan Shackleton have supported the project from the research stage through to publication: thank you both!

A special thank you to Ann Savours Shirley who has been very generous with her time in helping me with questions about *The South Polar Times*.

To those who have hosted me during the research and writing process: Naomi Bonham, Archivist at Scott Polar Research Institute for your great patience! Ivar Stokkeland & Anne-Britt Hinz at the Norsk Polarinstitutt, Tromsø.

I'm very grateful to all the poets and authors who have given me permission to quote from their works. I hope I have correctly credited you all in the Notes section.

I am grateful to Victoria Salem for giving me the idea for the Poetry at the Poles lecture, which then became this book.

Thank-you to the following: Delphine Aurès for pictures and potatoes; Rachel Morgan for giving me my first copy of *South*; Jeff Cox for help with Gerald Lysaght; Roddy Dunnet of the James Caird Society for help with photographs; Nico Beccalli; Elisabeth Griffith; Pauline Mayer; Felicity Aston.

Thank you to the Estate of Robert W. Service, in particular Anne Longepe, for permission to reproduce some his works.

Excerpts from diaries, papers, and correspondence held at SPRI and listed in the Notes section appear by permission of the University of Cambridge, Scott Polar Research Institute.

ABOUT THE AUTHOR

Jim Mayer has been travelling in the Arctic and Antarctic for many years and now works in the Polar Regions as an expedition leader and guide on small, adventurous cruise ships. His special interest is the history of polar exploration including both the well-known tales of the Heroic Age and obscure stories of marooned sailors and wartime spy missions.

Jim writes and presents lectures on the subject with titles including Poetry at the Poles, Scott; Shackleton and Amundsen: Which Leader Would You Follow?' and The War for the Weather. He attempted to ski the length of Svalbard from south to north but had to give up when all his food was eaten by polar bears. He also made the mistake of skiing 560 kilometres across the Greenland Icecap with a man he met in the pub.

BIBLIOGRAPHY & RESOURCES

BOOKS

Amundsen, Roald, (translated by A.G. Chater), *The South Pole*. London: C. Hurst, 1976.

Begbie, Harold, *Shackleton: A Memory*. London: Mills and Boon, 1922.

Bernacchi, Louis, *The Saga of the Discovery*. London: Blackie & Sons, 1928.

Browning, Robert, *Pocket Volume of Selections from The Poetical Works of Robert Browning*, London: Smith, Elder, 1891.

Carrington, Charles, *Rudyard Kipling, His Life and Work*. London: Macmillan, 1955.

Cherry-Garrard, Apsley, *The Worst Journey in the World*. London: Constable & Co., 1922.

Coles, Katharine, *The Earth Is Not Flat*. USA: Red Hen, 2013.

Daly, Regina W., *The Shackleton Letters – Behind the Scenes of the Nimrod Expedition*.

Norwich, UK: The Erskine Press, 2009.

Doorly, Gerald, *The Voyages of the Morning*. London: Smith, Elder, 1916.

Fiennes, Ranulph, *Captain Scott*. London: Coronet, 2003.

Fisher, Margery and James, *Shackleton*. London: Barrie, 1957.

Huntford, Roland, *Scott and Amundsen*. London: Pan, 1979.

Huntford, Roland, *Shackleton*. London: Cardinal, 1985.

Mill, Hugh Robert, *The Life of Sir Ernest Shackleton*. London: Heinemann, 1923.

Morrell, Margot and Stephanie Capparell: *Shackleton's Way*. London: Nicholas Brealey, 2001.

Moss, Sarah, *Scott's Last Biscuit: The Literature of Polar Exploration.*
Oxford: Signal, 2006.

Powter, Geoff, *We Cannot Fail.* London: Robinson, 2006.

Ralling, Christopher, *Shackleton.* London: BBC Books, 1983.

Rosove, Michael (ed.), *Rejoice My Heart, The Private Correspondence of Dr. Hugh Robert Mill and Lady Shackleton, 1922-33.* Santa Monica, USA: Adélie Books, 2007.

Savours, Ann, *The Voyages of the Discovery.* London: Virgin, 2000.

Savours, Ann, *Commentary (on the Folio Society edition of the South Polar Times).* London, Folio Society, 2012.

Scott, Robert, *The Voyage of the Discovery.* London: Murray, 1905.

Scott, Robert, (Huxley, Leonard, ed.), *Scott's Last Expedition.* London: Murray, 1913.

Seaver, George, *Edward Wilson of the Antarctic.* London: John Murray, 1936.

Simpson Housley, Paul, *Antarctica: Exploration, Perception and Metaphor.* London: Routledge, 1992.

Shackleton, Ernest, *"O.H.M.S." An Illustrated Record of the Voyage of S.S. "Tintagel Castle" from Southampton to Cape Town, March, 1900.* Recorded and illustrated by W. McLean & E. H. Shackleton. London: Simpkin & Marshall, 1900.

Shackleton, Ernest, *Aurora Australis.* Cape Royds, Antarctica: Printed at the Sign of the Penguins, 1908.

Shackleton, Ernest, *The Antarctic Book.* London: Heinemann, 1909.

Shackleton, Ernest, *Heart of the Antarctic.* London: Heinemann, 1909.

Shackleton, Ernest, *South.* London: Heinemann, 1919.

Spufford, Francis, *I Might Be Some Time.* London: Faber & Faber, 1996.

Thomas, Donald, Robert Browning, *A Life within a Life.* London: Weidenfeld & Nicholson, 1982.

Thomson, John, *Shackleton's Captain.* St. Leonards, NSW: Allen & Unwin, 1999.

Wheeler, Sara, Cherry, *A Life of Apsley Cherry-Garrard.* London:

Jonathan Cape, 2001.

Wilson, Edward, *Diary of the 'Discovery' Expedition to the Antarctic 1901-1904*.

London: Blandford Press, 1966.

Young, Louisa, *A Great Task of Happiness: The Life of Kathleen Scott*. London: Papermac, 1996.

ARTICLES

Karamanski, Theodore J, "The Heroic Ideal: Romantic Literature and the British Exploration of the Antarctic, 1901-1914." *The Journal of Polar Studies*, Vol. 1(2): 461-469.

Mills, Leif, "Polar Friction." http://website.lineone.net/~polar. publishing/polarfriction.pdf, accessed June 2014.

Piggot, Jan, "Shackleton Reader and Writer." Dulwich, London: *Journal of the James Caird Society*.

Unknown Author, "How I Began." London: *The Captain*, Vol.23 (133).

RESOURCES

www.jamescairdsociety.com

The *James Caird Society*, established in 1994 and a registered charity, is the only institution that exists to preserve the memory and honour the remarkable feats of Sir Ernest Shackleton.

www.spri.cam.ac.uk/library/archives/shackleton/

This website, part of the library at the Scott Polar Research Institute, "allows you to view a selection of our archive and museum treasures and aims to provide a scholarly resource [on all Shackleton matters] as well as an introduction to the Institute's wealth of historical documents and artifacts."

www.antarctic-circle.org

The *Antarctic Circle* is a non-commercial forum and resource on historical, literary, bibliographical, artistic and cultural aspects of Antarctica and the South Polar Regions.

www.enduranceobituaries.co.uk

A super website detailing what happened to the men of Shackleton's expeditions once they returned home.

NOTES

INTRODUCTION

1. Recorded by Albert Armitage, reported in Fisher, Margery and James, *Shackleton*. London: Barrie, 1957

2. *The Times,* 28 October 1911

3. Shackleton's Diary, Scott Polar Research Institute, Cambridge (hereafter SPRI) MS 1537/3/9 3 January 1922

2. EARLY YEARS

4. *The Captain,* 1910, vol. 23

5. Mill, Hugh Robert, *The Life of Sir Ernest Shackleton.* London: Heinemann, 1923. p5

6. *The Captain, op cit*

7. *Ibid*

8. SPRI MS 100/91/1

9. SPRI MS 1456/74:D

10. Hanson, Neil, *The Custom of the Sea.* London: Doubleday, 1999. p202

11. Mill, H.R., *The Life of Sir Ernest Shackleton.* London: Heinemann, 1923. p52

12. Letter to Emily SPRI MS 1537/2/31/6

13. *The Captain, op. cit*

14. Letter to Emily, 15 August 1924

15. *Ibid*

3. EMILY

16. Letter from Emily to H. R. Mill, 25 May 1922, in Rosove, Michael (ed.), *Rejoice my Heart, The Private Correspondence of Dr. Hugh Robert*

Mill and Lady Shackleton, 1922-33. Santa Monica, California: Adélie Books, 2007.

17. SPRI MS 1537 2/4/2
18. *Ibid*
19. Letter from Emily to H. R. Mill, 9 January 1923, in Rosove, *op. cit*
20. *Ibid*
21. *Ibid*, 28 June 1922
22. *Ibid*, 21 May 1922
23. Armitage, Albert B., Letter to H. R. Mill, 24 May 1922, SPRI
24. Letter from Emily to H. R. Mill, 8 June 1922 in Rosove, *op cit*
25. SPRI MS, 12 August 1898
26. Armitage, Albert B., letter to H. R. Mill, 20 May 1922
27. Mill, H.R., *The Life of Sir Ernest Shackleton*. p51
28. SPRI MS: 1537/2/5/3:D, 3 August 1901

4. NEMO JOINS *DISCOVERY*

29. Letter to Charles Dorman, 3 August 1901, SPRI
30. Shackleton Diary, 25 January 1902
31. Shackleton Diary, 1 February 1902
32. Shackleton Diary, 8 February 1902
33. Thomas, Donald, *Robert Browning, A Life Within a Life*. London: Weidenfeld & Nicholson, 1982. p171
34. Armitage, Albert, 1905, quoted in Fisher, Margery & James, *Shackleton*. p41
35. Huntford, Roland, *Shackleton*. p75
36. Wilson, Edward, *Diary of the 'Discovery' Expedition to the Antarctic 1901-1904*. London: Blandford Press, 1966. p131
37. Shackleton to Emily Dorman, 20 April 1901

5. ULYSSES RETURNS

38. Moss, Sarah, *Scott's Last Biscuit: The Literature of Polar Exploration*. Oxford: Signal, 2006. p25
39. *The Referee*, quoted in Huntford, Roland, *Shackleton*, but unusually

for Huntford not referenced

40. Shackleton Diary, 2 January 1903

41. Seaver, George, *Edward Wilson of the Antarctic*. London: John Murray, 1936. p102

42. *Ibid*, p102

43. Shackleton Diary, 11 Jan 1903

44. Shackleton, Ernest, *South*. London: Heinemann, 1919. p129

45. Wilson, Edward, *Diary*, 14 January 1903

46. *Ibid*, 24 January 1903

47. *Ibid*

48. Seaver, George, *Edward Wilson of the Antarctic.* p114

49. Wilson, Edward, *Diary*, 3 February 1903

50. Doorly, Gerald, *The Voyages of the Morning.* London: Smith, Elder, 1916

51. Wilson, Edward, *Diary*, 4- 24 February 1903

52. Wilson, Edward, *Diary*, 14 January 1903

53. Cherry-Garrard, Apsley, *The Worst Journey in the World*. London: Constable & Co., 1922. p477

6. "L'Envoi"

54. *The South Polar Times*, vol. 6, April 1903

55. Quoted in Wilson, Edward, *Diary*, June 1902

56. *Ibid*, 12 May 1902

7. Coming Home

57. *Songs of the Morning, A Musical Sketch* (CD Recording, 2002, UKAHT) based on The Songs of the Morning by Doorly, Bread and Cheese Club, Melbourne (1943) SPRI Library (7)91(08)

58. *Ibid*

59. Wells, H. G., *Anticipations of the Reaction of Mechanical and Scientific Progress upon Human Life and Thought*. London: Chapman and Hall, 1901. p103

60. SPRI MS 1456/26

8. MARRIED LIFE

61. SPRI MS 1456/26 30 May 1922

62. SPRI MS 1537, 26 February 1904

63. Letter from Emily to H. R. Mill, 2 June 1922, in Rosove, *op. cit*

64. *New York Times*, 1 May 1910

65. SPRI Shackleton letter to Emily, 11 January 1904

66. Shackleton, Alexandra, Preface to Rosove, *op. cit*

67. Mill, H. R., *The Life of Sir Ernest Shackleton*. p90

68. *Ibid*, p97

69. Armitage, Albert B., Letter to H. R. Mill, 24 May 1922, SPRI

70. Letter from Emily to H. R. Mill, 27 May 1922

71. *New York Tribune,* 3 April 1910

72. SPRI Letter from Emily to H. R. Mill, 22 October 1922

73. SPRI MS:100/104/1-66: 22.10.1922

74. *Ibid*, 16 August 1922

9. *NIMROD*

75. *Daily Telegraph*, 12 June 1909

76. Quoted in Mill, H. R., *The Life of Sir Ernest Shackleton*. p98

77. *The Times*, 12 February 1907

78. SPRI MS 1456/25, 15 February 1908

79. See Spufford, Francis: *I Might Be Some Time*. London: Faber & Faber, 1996. pp83-85

80. Shackleton, Ernest, *Heart of the Antarctic*. p185 (Extracted from Shackleton's diary of 20 November 1908) (Shackleton also uses the verse in *South*, p173)

81. Shackleton, Ernest. *South*. 1919. p120

82. Simpson Housley, Paul; Antarctica: *Exploration, Perception and Metaphor*. London: Routledge, 1992. p114

83. Vilhjalmur Stefannson

84. Shackleton, Ernest, *Heart of the Antarctic*. p185 (Extracted from Shackleton's diary of 20 November 1908)

85. *Ibid*, p185

86. SPRI MS 1537/2/16/3 Letter to Emily, 26 Jan 1908

87. *Ibid*

88. SPRI MS 1537/3/11 BJ

10. TINY BLACK SPECKS

89. SPRI MS1537/2/16/3, Letter to Emily, 26 Jan 1908

90. Shackleton, Ernest, *Heart of the Antarctic.* p224

91. Eric Marshall, letter to Dudley Everitt, 23 January 1956, at RGS

92. *Op. cit*, 17 June 1908

93. Shackleton, Ernest, *Heart of the Antarctic.* p191

94. *Ibid*

95. *Ibid*

96. SPRI Emily Shackleton, letter to H. R. Mill, 16 August 1922

97. Quoted in the *Daily Mail*, 26 March 1909

98. Mill, H. R., *The Life of Ernest Shackleton.* p245

99. Quoted in Thomson, John, *Shackleton's Captain.* St. Leonards, NSW: Allen & Unwin, 1999. pp189-193

100. Saunders, Edward, Letter to H. R. Mill, 1922

101. Karamanski, Theodore J., "The Heroic Ideal: Romantic Literature and the British Exploration of the Antarctic, 1901-1914." *The Journal of Polar Studies*, Vol. 1(2): 461-469

11. "THE LONE TRAIL"

102. Voices of History 2, CD British Library NSACD19-20 issued 2005 & http://www.youtube.com/watch?v=OUTHZ_9tacM accessed June 2013

103. Klinck, Carl F., *Robert Service: A Biography.* New York: Dodd, Mead, 1976

104. *Ibid*

105. *Aftenposten* (British Library Newspapers), 16 October 1909

106. Amundsen, Roald: *The South Pole*, translation by A. G. Chater. London: C. Hurst, 1976. p41

107. Mill, H. R., The Life of Sir Ernest Shackleton. p166
108. SPRI MS 100/75/1-26 D
109. Mill, H. R., The Life of Sir Ernest Shackleton. p166
110. SPRI MS 100/75/1-26 D
111. Mawson, Douglas: Home of the Blizzard. London: Heinemann, 1915. Chapter XIII
112. Letter from Emily Shackleton to H. R. Mill, October 7 1922
113. Shackleton: A Description of the Dash for the South Pole. British Library recording, 23 June 1909
114. Pearson's Magazine, vol. 38 (224), 1914

12. SOUTH

115. The Times, 30 December 1913.
116. National Maritime Museum, Greenwich, (hereafter NMM) MS FI.L962-L952
117. The Evening Post, Vol. LXXV Issue 21, 25 January 1908
118. SPRI MS 367/4/1 Saunders, Edward, Letter to H. R. Mill, 1922
119. SPRI MS 1537/2/32 1-2
120. Shackleton, Ernest, South. p83
121. Job, Chapter 38 v 3
122. Rex, Tamiko (ed.), South with Endurance: The Photographs of Frank Hurley. London: Bloomsbury, 2001. p89
123. Hurley, Frank, Shackleton's Argonauts. London: Angus & Robertson, 1948. p80
124. Shackleton, Ernest, South. p182
125. Mill, H. R., The Life of Sir Ernest Shackleton. p245
126. Ibid, p245
127. Shackleton, Ernest, South. p202
128. Ibid, p205
129. Thomson, John, Shackleton's Captain. Toronto: Mosaic Press, 1999. p99
130. Shackleton, Ernest: South. p209
131. Quoted in Morrell and Capparell, Shackleton's Way. London:

Nicholas Brealey, 2001

132. Fisher, Margery and James, *Shackleton*, Appendix B

133. T.S. Eliot, Notes to *The Waste Land*, line 360. The Notes were not included with the first publications of *The Waste Land*, but were added from December 1922

13. THE GREAT WAR

134. De Micheli, Luciano (cello soloist), unpublished diary. Translated from *Dalla Terra del Fuoco al Montello (From Tierra del Fuego to Montello)* by De Micheli's great neice, for the author

135. *Ibid*

136. From *The Times Literary Supplement*, quoted in Sassoon's diary (May 1917) and later Shackleton

137. Shackleton, Ernest, *South*. p210

138. Ricketts, Harry, *Strange Meetings: The Poets of the Great War*. London: Chatto & Windus, 2010. p202

139. Shackleton, Ernest: Speech in Sydney, Australia, 20 March 1917, quoted in Mill, H. R., *The Life of Sir Ernest Shackleton*

140. Marr, Andrew: *My Trade: A Short History of British Journalism*. London: Macmillan, 2004

141. SPRI MS: 100/110/2 26 October 1918

142. SPRI MS 100/108: D

143. SPRI MS1456/93: D

144. Birch-Jones, A. F., letter to James and Margery Fisher, quoted in Huntford, Roland, *Shackelton*. The original letter seems to be missing from the Fisher papers at SPRI

145. Mill, H. R., *The Life of Sir Ernest Shackleton*. p264

146. Emily Shackleton, letter to H. R. Mill, 22 October 1922

14. *QUEST*

147. SPRI MS 1537/3/7, Shackleton Diary, 23 December 1915

148. Emily Shackleton, Letter to H. R. Mill, 1 July 1922

149. SPRI MS: 100/50/1-6 D: J. A. Hussey letter to H. R. Mill, 27 July 1922

150. SPRI MS 100/96 Letter to H. R. Mill

151. SPRI MS 1603/92: D

152. *Pearson's Weekly*, 8 April 1909

153. NMM PVS/9

154. Fisher, Margery and James, *Shackleton*. p135

15. "PROSPICE"

155. *The Captain*, April 1910

156. *The Times*, 23 August 1880

157. *The Times*, 28 January 1887

158. Quoted in Begbie, Harold, *Shackleton: A Memory.* London: Mills and Boon, 1922

159. Emily Shackleton, letter to H. R. Mill, 8 June 1922

160. SPRI MS 1537/2/12/21

161. SPRI MS 1456/25

162. Emily Shackleton, letter to H. R. Mill, 8 December 1922

163. NMM 820-1:094

16. SHACKLETON'S LAST VERSE

164. SPRI MS 1647

165. SPRI MS 1537/3/9

166. SPRI MS 1537/2/12/21, 27 August 1907

17. "THE STATUE AND THE BUST"

167. SPRI MS 1456/93

168. NMM /IVR/8 (2)

169. The full poem is to be found in the anthology *Poems for a Machine Age*, edited by Horace J. McNeil. London: McGraw-Hill Book Co., 1959

170. Manhire, Bill, Introduction to *The Wide White Page*, Victoria, Australia: Victoria University Press, 2004

171. NMM: IVR/11, letter to Elspeth Beardmore, 13 January 1914

172. Letter to H. R. Mill, 27 August 1922

173. SPRI MS 1537/2/12/18: D
174. Letter to H. R. Mill, 30 May 1922
175. Letter to Leonard Tripp, 23 March 1922, quoted in Huntford, Roland, *Shackleton*

18. THE LOST POEM

176. SPRI MS 1537/2/25/18
177. SPRI MS 1537/2/25/5
178. From the album *Saltrubbed Eyes*, 1993
179. SPRI MS 1603/3/1

19. SHACKLETON'S LEGACY

180. Quoted in Morrell, Margot and Stephanie Capparell, *Shackleton's Way*
181. *New York Times*, 1 May 1910
182. Begbie, Harold, *Shackleton: A Memory*

INDEX